Matthew *for* Young People

Matthew *for* Young People

CATE DAVIS

RESOURCE *Publications* · Eugene, Oregon

MATTHEW FOR YOUNG PEOPLE

Copyright © 2022 Cate Davis. All rights reserved. Except for brief quotations in critical publications or reviews, no part of this book may be reproduced in any manner without prior written permission from the publisher. Write: Permissions, Wipf and Stock Publishers, 199 W. 8th Ave., Suite 3, Eugene, OR 97401.

Resource Publications
An Imprint of Wipf and Stock Publishers
199 W. 8th Ave., Suite 3
Eugene, OR 97401

www.wipfandstock.com

PAPERBACK ISBN: 978-1-6667-3418-8
HARDCOVER ISBN: 978-1-6667-2977-1
EBOOK ISBN: 978-1-6667-2978-8

MARCH 21, 2022 11:48 AM

All Scripture quotations, unless otherwise indicated, are taken from the Holy Bible, New International Version®, NIV®. Copyright ©1973, 1978, 1984, 2011 by Biblica, Inc.™ Used by permission of Zondervan. All rights reserved worldwide. www.zondervan.comThe "NIV" and "New International Version" are trademarks registered in the United States Patent and Trademark Office by Biblica, Inc.™

For Hudson.
Because God's steadfast love is better than life.

Contents

Series Preface | *xi*
Introduction to the Gospel of Matthew | *xv*

Day 1	The Genealogy of Jesus	1
Day 2	The Birth of Jesus	4
Day 3	The Wise Men	8
Day 4	The Escape to Egypt	12
Day 5	John the Baptist — Part 1	16
Day 6	John the Baptist — Part 2	20
Day 7	Jesus in the Wilderness	23
Day 8	Jesus Calls His Disciples	27
Day 9	The Beatitudes — Part 1	31
Day 10	The Beatitudes — Part 2	35
Day 11	Righteousness	40
Day 12	What's Going on in Your Heart?	44
Day 13	Seek First His Kingdom and Righteousness	48
Day 14	A Warning and a Promise	53
Day 15	Opposite Paths	57
Day 16	Jesus' Healing Ministry	61

Day 17	Being a Disciple	65
Day 18	God's Upside Down Values	69
Day 19	A Compassionate God	73
Day 20	The First Missionaries	77
Day 21	Take up Your Cross	81
Day 22	An Angry Warning and a Tender Invitation	86
Day 23	Jesus, the Christ	91
Day 24	Watch Your Tongue	94
Day 25	The Parable of the Sower	98
Day 26	The Kingdom of Heaven — Part 1	102
Day 27	The Kingdom of Heaven — Part 2	105
Day 28	A Day in the Life of Jesus — Part 1	109
Day 29	A Day in the Life of Jesus — Part 2	112
Day 30	Cultural Traditions vs. God's Word	116
Day 31	True Worship	121
Day 32	Understanding Spiritual Truths	124
Day 33	The Transfiguration	128
Day 34	A Mustard Seed of Faith	132
Day 35	Lessons From Children	136
Day 36	Angels and Sheep	140
Day 37	Forgiveness	143
Day 38	Marriage	147
Day 39	The Rich and the Kingdom of God	151
Day 40	The Offensive Gospel of Grace	155

Day 41	The Greatness of a Servant	159
Day 42	Jesus the King	163
Day 43	Warnings for the Self-Righteous	167
Day 44	The Wedding Banquet – Part 1	171
Day 45	The Wedding Banquet — Part 2	175
Day 46	The Greatest Commandment — Part 1	178
Day 47	The Greatest Commandment — Part 2	182
Day 48	The Greatest Commandment — Part 3	186
Day 49	The Greatest Commandment — Part 4	190
Day 50	The Second Greatest Commandment — Part 1	194
Day 51	The Second Greatest Commandment — Part 2	198
Day 52	Don't Be a Pharisee — Part 1	203
Day 53	Don't Be a Pharisee — Part 2	207
Day 54	Keep Watch	211
Day 55	Parables about Being Prepared	215
Day 56	The Sheep and the Goats	219
Day 57	The Perfume and the Plot	223
Day 58	The Last Supper and the Garden of Gethsemane	227
Day 59	Jesus is Always Faithful	231
Day 60	Pilate and Barabbas	235
Day 61	The Crucifixion	239
Day 62	The Importance of Jesus' Death	243
Day 63	The Resurrected King	247

Bibliography | 251

Series Preface

ALL AROUND US PEOPLE are living restless lives, searching everywhere for contentment but never quite finding it. They're always on the move, flitting from one love to another, seeking meaning and purpose. They're constantly changing what they buy, what they look like, what they do, who they're with, where they are. And yet the ache for something more never quite goes away.

If you're tired of the endless searching, and long for a deeply rooted life, the Bible is the exact right place to be.

It's where you'll find joy that fills your heart right up to overflowing.
It's where you'll find hope that never fails.
It's where you'll find an identity that can't be taken away from you.
It's where you'll find the steadfast love your heart aches for.
It's where you'll find rest.

Not because the Bible is all about you. But because the Bible is where we get to know God. The Bible is God's story. It's about who he is and what he's done. And inside the story of God is where we find out who we are, and what life is all about. Inside God's story is where we're given the freedom and safety to finally set down our roots in a firm foundation that will never disappoint us.

The Bible is also the main way God speaks to us, teaching us, encouraging us, challenging us, transforming us, and empowering us. But it can be really hard to know where to start reading the Bible. Even once we do start reading, it can sometimes be confusing and difficult to understand. The Growing Roots series is designed to help you read the Bible for yourself, one book at a time. Studying whole books of the Bible is really important so that we can hear God's full message to us, instead of focusing on just the most famous verses and topics. It shapes our understanding of the whole Bible as one beautiful picture of who our amazing God is.

Series Preface

Developing a daily rhythm of reading through whole books of the Bible will also help your spiritual roots grow deep and strong. Plants don't grow healthy roots instantly. They develop slowly, day by day, bit by bit. The stronger they grow over time, the more they're able to bring life to the plant above. In Psalm 1, people who enjoy God's Word every day are described as being "like a tree planted by streams of water", leafy and fruitful and flourishing. This has been my prayer over you as I write: that as you go deep into the Bible each day, your faith will grow more alive and rich. That your love-relationship with God will blossom beautifully, just like a tree with deep roots that's planted next to a life-giving stream. That through his Word, God will nourish and sustain you, deeply refreshing you and satisfying you in a way you never imagined could be possible.

Reading the Bible and praying every day isn't always easy, but the best things in life are never the easiest things. And I promise you: it will be abundantly, overwhelmingly, gloriously worth the effort. Walking closely with God every day is the best thing you'll ever do. Jesus promises that when we seek him we'll find him. And Jesus *always* keeps his promises. So keep making the choice to invest your precious time today and tomorrow and every day after that in the only thing that really matters: knowing God. Pursue him. Run after him as if your life depends on it. Because it does. And you know what? He's already pursuing you, waiting for you with open arms and love in his eyes.

> *Then you will call upon me and pray to me*
> *And I will listen to you.*
> *You will seek me and find me*
> *When you seek me with all your heart.*
> *(Jeremiah 29:12–13)*

Series Preface

How to use this book

What you'll need:

- Some alone time in a quiet place, preferably at the start of each new day.
- Your Bible. In this book I quote the NIV, but you can you use any version.
- This devotional book.
- A journal to write your thoughts and notes in (optional).
- A pen or pencil.

The process:

1. *Prayer.*

    We should always start our time with God in humble prayer. Ask God to open your heart and mind to be able to understand what you're about to read. Ask that he would show you more of who he is, and who he made you to be. Pray that he would be honored by your desire to get to know him.

2. *Bible.*

    In your Bible, read the verses indicated at the top of the page in this devotional book. Feel free read it more than once, and even to write notes in the margins or underline things as you go. I always find that helps me remember the most interesting and important things later on.

3. *Study notes.*

    Read the notes on the Bible passage in this devotional book. Once again, it can be helpful to write your thoughts in the margins, or underline interesting things as you go.

4. *Reflection questions.*

    Answer the reflection questions at the end of the devotional notes, using your journal if you want to write your answers down. Take your time to really think them through, and answer honestly. This is not a test; no one will be reading or judging your answers afterwards. They're for you alone, to help you think carefully and deeply about how to apply what you've just read in God's Word to your own life.

5. *Prayer.*

Talk to God about what you read. You can use the prayer at the end of the reflection questions, or you can pray whatever's in your own heart. Or you can do both!

6. *Meditation.*

A Bible verse is provided for you to meditate on throughout the day. Christian meditation means to think carefully about, dwell on, pray through, and reflect on what God has revealed about himself in the Bible. The meditation verse will be short, but it will remind you of one of the key ideas from your devotions. Keep a photo of it on your phone, or write it on your hand or on a small notecard in your wallet, so that you can keep focusing on it as you go through your day.

Introduction to the Gospel of Matthew

Every book in the Bible was written by a human being, but inspired by the Holy Spirit. How this works exactly is one of the amazing mysteries of God, but it means the Bible you have in front of you is 100 percent the words of God and 100 percent the words of the human authors who wrote it. Each book also has its own unique genre (style and structure), and original audience, and it's important that we understand a bit of that context around the book of Matthew before we start reading.

Who wrote it:	This book was written by Jesus' disciple Matthew, a tax collector also known as Levi. Matthew was an eyewitness to all of the events in the last three years of Jesus' life.
When it was written:	Experts believe it was written between 17 and 37 years after Jesus' death.
Genre:	Gospel. This means it's a story of the life of Jesus, based on eye-witness accounts, and that it also includes long examples of Jesus' teachings and sermons.
Original audience:	This Gospel was originally written for early Christians who had Jewish heritage, probably living in Syria.

Day 1

The Genealogy of Jesus

(Read Matthew 1:1–17)

The book of Matthew begins with Jesus' genealogy, which is the record of his family's history. At first glance, this is just a long, boring list of names. Just remember though: nothing is in the Bible by accident, so there must be something important for us to learn about Jesus in this passage.

Jesus was a real historical person

This list of Jesus' ancestors is included in the Bible to show us very clearly that Jesus is not a made-up character. He's not a fictional superhero. He has a well-known, historically accurate family history. By listing some of Jesus' relatives at the start of his book, Matthew is showing his readers – who were originally Christians of Jewish descent – that Jesus' story is rooted firmly in history, not in folklore or legend. He's challenging us to take the story we're reading seriously, and to believe that the events he wrote down actually did happen.

Not only does this list of names show us that Jesus was a real historical person, but it also shows us he was a direct relative of two of the most well-known and respected people in Jewish history: Abraham and King David. In ancient Jewish culture, your family was your identity. People were known by who they were related to, and a family's reputation was extremely important. Matthew's ancient Jewish readers would have respected Jesus based on his impressive family connections.

Jesus can use anyone to be part of his amazing story

You might not have noticed it, but this list of names includes four women. Tamar, Rahab, Ruth, and the wife of Uriah (whose name was Bathsheba). This might not seem very unusual to us, but in ancient Jewish culture women weren't normally included in genealogies because they weren't considered to be equal to men. So this must be something special!

If we dig a little deeper, things get even more mysterious. These women have very unusual stories: Tamar tricked her father-in-law into getting her pregnant by pretending to be a prostitute (Genesis 38); Rahab was a prostitute (Joshua 2); Ruth was a poor widow and an outsider from a different cultural and religious group (Ruth 1); and Bathsheba was seduced by King David before he killed her husband Uriah so he could marry her (2 Samuel 11). That's quite a controversial family tree!

So why are these particular women's names singled out in Jesus' genealogy? Matthew uses these four women to remind us that no matter who we are, what we've done, or what we've been through, God still has a great plan for our lives. Just look at Jesus' own heritage! God was in complete control of when and where Jesus was born into human history. He could have chosen to only have the holiest and most respectable people in Jesus' family tree, but instead he deliberately included people who the rest of society might ignore or look down on. Not only are they women in a male-centered culture, but they're poor women, immigrant women, women with questionable morals, women who had survived trauma and abuse by powerful men.

This is great news for every single one of us! We all make bad choices. Little secret ones every day and big horrible ones that have the potential to ruin our lives and the lives of the people around us. But God loves us in spite of our mess, and offers to forgive us. Many of us have had terrible things done to us. We've been hated and rejected and treated as if we're worthless. But God honors the value in every human being. He treasures us, and invites us to be adopted into his family and to become part of his amazing story.

Hebrews 2:11 says, "Jesus is not ashamed to call them brothers and sisters." Soak in the truth of that for a moment and let your heart be encouraged by it. He is not ashamed of you. He is not embarrassed to call you his own. He doesn't regret loving you. He's chosen you specifically. He promises that no matter how badly your life has gone up until now, he can make the mess into something beautiful. No matter how terrible you think you are, he can use you to glorify his name. No matter how badly other people treat you, he thinks you're valuable and special, and he has a role in his story designed just for you.

Reflect and respond

1. *How do you feel knowing that God chose prostitutes and murderers and outsiders to be in Jesus' family tree? How do you feel knowing that he isn't ashamed to call you his family too?*
2. *Why can it be hard for you to believe that God wants to make something beautiful out of your messy life?*

Dear God,
Thank you that you're real.
Thank you that Jesus was a real historical person.
Thank you that you have a place in your beautiful story for hurting, messy people like Tamar, Rahab, Ruth, Bathsheba, and me.
Please help me trust that you have a wonderful plan for my life.

In Jesus' name,
Amen

Meditation verse for the day:

Jesus is not ashamed to call
them brothers and sisters.
(Hebrews 2:11)

Day 2

The Birth of Jesus

(Read Matthew 1:18–25)

Maybe you were confused when you read this story of Jesus' birth. Where was the donkey? And the little town of Bethlehem? And wasn't there meant to be a manger in there somewhere? There are actually four books in the Bible that tell us about Jesus' life: Matthew, Mark, Luke and John. They're called the Gospels – which means 'good news' – and they are each slightly different because they're written from different perspectives. For example, Mark and John don't tell us anything at all about Jesus' birth, and Matthew doesn't include as many details about it as Luke does. If you're interested in reading the version with the manger and the shepherds and the host of angels, you can read all about it in Luke 2.

But are you still wondering why the two versions of Jesus' birth are not exactly the same? It might help to think about it like this: if you and your friend went to the zoo and were telling someone else about it afterwards, would you both tell the story in the exact same way with the exact same details? There's no way. You might talk mostly about the elephants and how the weather was hot, and your friend might focus on the orangutans and the delicious ice-cream she ate.

Just because your stories aren't identical, does that mean one of you is wrong? Does it mean that you're lying about going to the zoo together? Of course not. They are simply two versions of the same event, told from two different perspectives.

The Birth of Jesus

The Gospels always describe events slightly differently, because they're based on eye-witness accounts from a variety of people. As we know, everyone focuses on different parts of the event they're observing. The Gospels were also written for different audiences, so with the leading of the Holy Spirit, their authors picked the specific parts of Jesus' life and teaching that were most important for their audience to know about. Because Matthew's audience was mainly Christians who had Jewish family roots, he focuses heavily on events in Jesus' life that connect to his Jewish heritage. Matthew is particularly careful to highlight the fact that Jesus is the Jewish Messiah. *Messiah* means 'Chosen One' in Hebrew, the Jewish language.

Mary and Joseph

Let's focus on Mary and Joseph for a moment: they were a poor couple from a small country town, who were engaged to be married. Back in those days, peasant girls got married any time after the age of about twelve, so Mary was probably a young teenager and Joseph might have been just a bit older. Think about how a pregnant, unmarried teenage girl would probably have been treated in that traditional little town. It's unlikely that many people believed her miraculous story, or showed her any respect. People must have gossiped about her behind her back, and other parents might not have wanted their daughters to be friends with her. Her own family might have been ashamed of her!

As for Joseph, how do you think he felt being told by an angel to go ahead and marry a woman who was pregnant with a child that wasn't his? I'm sure he felt hurt and confused, and maybe even angry. He must have wondered if he could trust Mary and the angel. He definitely would have been tempted to just leave her and find someone else to marry. In fact, legally at that time he could have even had Mary stoned to death for adultery!

But Joseph had the courage to trust and obey the angel's instructions and he stood by Mary, raising Jesus as if he were his own son. Because of this hard, brave decision, he had the privilege of becoming part of the greatest story in human history. Imagine if he'd given in to the temptation to take the easy path out of the relationship. Someone else would have become Jesus' step-dad instead of him! He would have missed the opportunity to care for the most special little boy ever born on earth, the Savior of the world. Do you think you would have had the faith to trust God's plan and risk being laughed at or rejected by your entire community?

God could have chosen for his precious Son to be born into a rich family, or even a royal family. He could have been born into a family in Rome, the most powerful city on earth at the time. Instead, Jesus was born to a couple of poor teenagers who lived in a country town in the middle of nowhere. Isn't it just amazing that the King of kings and Lord of lords would humble himself like that just for us? By choosing Mary and Joseph, God is also sending us a clear message that he doesn't judge people by the world's standards. He doesn't care if we're rich or attractive or powerful or popular. He doesn't care if no one around us thinks we're valuable. He knows us and loves us, and he has a purpose for our lives that's beyond our wildest dreams. All he asks is that we trust and obey him.

The humble birth

The most incredible thing about Jesus' birth is not actually that Mary was a virgin, even though that gets a lot of attention. The most mind-blowing thing about Jesus' birth is that God became human. This is called the incarnation. In verse 23, one of the names given to Jesus is Immanuel, which means 'God with us.' Think about that for a moment! God came to be with us!

This is the real beauty of Christmas: that the helpless little baby lying in that manger is the magnificent Creator of all things.

He left heaven for us.

He gave up being equal with God for us.

He lay down his divine glory for us.

He lowered himself from creating galaxies to being a sleepy, poop-filled blob who couldn't even hold his own head up.

All out of love for us.

What a God!

Don't leave it until Christmas each year to marvel at this reality. Every time you see a baby, remember baby Jesus and let awe awaken in your heart. He was a real little human child. He was God come to earth to be with us. Standing with us in the fire. With us through the flood. With us in the middle of the messes we make of things. With us in the best and worst moments of our lives. We have a God who cares about us so deeply that he made a way to be with us. And he'll never leave us or forsake us. Let it never stop amazing you! Let it never stop leading you to worship him!

The Birth of Jesus

Reflect and respond

1. *What does this passage teach/remind you about who God is?*
2. *Joseph was probably confused and terrified, but he chose to trust and obey God anyway. What makes trusting and obeying God hard for you?*

Father God,
Thank you that nothing in this universe is too hard for you, like creating the stars in the sky, or making a virgin pregnant.
Thank you that you love me so much you sent me Jesus, your precious Son.
Thank you for the humility and compassion Jesus showed by becoming human.
I'm sorry that I sometimes struggle to trust your plan.
Please give me the courage to trust you and obey you like Joseph did, so that I can play my part in the amazing story that you have planned for my life.

In Jesus' name,
Amen

Meditation verse for the day:

"The virgin will conceive and give birth to a son,
and they will call him Immanuel"
(which means, "God with us").
(Matthew 1:23)

Day 3

The Wise Men

(Read Matthew 2:1–12)

What picture do you have in your head of the wise men who visit baby Jesus? Let me guess: There are three of them, and they're holding gifts and bowing to Jesus (who is in the manger), alongside the shepherds and lots of animals. Right? But is that actually what the Bible is telling us happened? Read the passage again carefully to check.

Looking closely at the text

Firstly, the wise men definitely bring three gifts, but does that mean there are three of them, like we usually assume? We don't actually know. All we know is that the Greek word used to describe them is plural, so there was definitely more than one wise man. But there could have been two, or there could have been thirty, or even more!

Secondly, every Christmas nativity scene is probably wrong, because it's not likely the wise men visited Jesus at the exact same time as the shepherds. Luke 2 tells us that the shepherds were at the stable on the night of Jesus' birth, but we really don't know exactly when the wise men came. There are a few clues in this passage, however:

- *Clue #1:* In one translation of the Bible, verse 1 says the wise men arrived "about that time" but not necessarily on that exact night. In some other translations, it says that the wise men visited King Herod in Jerusalem "after Jesus was born", which means they wouldn't have made it all the way from Jerusalem to Bethlehem on the same night he was born.

- *Clue #2:* Verse 11 says the wise men worshipped Jesus at a house. So, we know for sure that by the time the wise men arrived in Bethlehem, Jesus' family had moved from the stable where he was born into a house.
- *Clue #3:* Verse 16 explains that the wise men told King Herod the star had first appeared two whole years beforehand. We don't know if the star first appeared as soon as Jesus was born, or if it appeared before his actual birth, but this does tell us that Jesus could have been anywhere up to around two years old by the time the wise men reached him.

Why does it even matter?

After all that, you might be wondering why it really matters how many wise men there were, or when exactly they visited baby Jesus. Honestly, it doesn't matter much. The main point here is just to show that we sometimes get caught up believing things about Jesus that are not in the Bible. Our culture or church traditions might teach us something that's completely different from what the Bible actually says! The Bible is the Word of God, and it's trustworthy. Anything else that your pastor says, or that you hear from your family, or that you read online or in a book (including this one!) might be teaching you something about God that just isn't true. This is really, really dangerous. If we don't read the Bible carefully for ourselves and test everything we hear against it, we can easily start believing things that the Bible never actually says. We can end up following a religion that's called Christianity, but doesn't actually look anything like what we find in the Bible.

Eyes of faith

But who actually were these wise men? The Greek word *magoi* which we translate to mean 'wise men' probably meant something like 'astrologers' or 'philosophers.' Sometimes they've even been called 'kings'. Whoever they were, we know from verse 1 that they travelled all the way from lands in the east, which probably means places like Persia, India, or Babylon.

So try to imagine this: a group of well-educated, respectable, wealthy men, pack up some very expensive gifts and travel to a house in a small village, where they bow down before a little boy born to a couple of poor teenage peasants who were from a totally different culture and religion from them. What a bizarre thing to do! I wonder if they felt a little bit silly. Or maybe they were so sure this child was someone special, that they felt like this was the only logical response. Many people might have looked at Jesus and just seen another little kid. But these men looked at Jesus and saw someone worth worshipping.

We need to pray to be able see life through the eyes of faith, just like these wise men did. Faith mean boldly trusting in what we can't see yet. The Holy Spirit helps us look past the physical world around us, into the hidden spiritual reality that's deeper, truer, and more real than anything here on earth. Instead of focusing on a random bad thing that just happened to us, the eyes of faith help us see the deeper reality that God is still in control of it all, sitting on his eternal throne. Instead of wondering where God has gone when he feels far away, the eyes of faith help us see that he's always with us and will never leave us. Instead of seeing Jesus as just an interesting historical figure, the eyes of faith help us see that he is the King of kings, worthy of all our worship.

Reflect and respond

1. *Why do you think it's important to personally know what the Bible says, instead of just believing whatever other people tell you is true?*
2. *Why do you sometimes struggle to believe Jesus is worthy of all your worship?*

Lord,
Thank you for giving me the Bible so I can read about who you say you are.
Thank you that you want me to get to know you personally.
Lord, the wise men weren't ashamed to bow down before little baby Jesus even though it might have looked ridiculous to other people.
Please give me the eyes of faith, so that I can see who you really are.
I want to live a life that honors and worships you in the way you deserve.

In Jesus' name,
Amen

The Wise Men

Meditation verse for the day:

At the name of Jesus every knee should bow,
in heaven and on earth and under the earth.
(Philippians 2:10)

Day 4

The Escape to Egypt

(Read Matthew 2:13–23)

History is filled with terribly sad events, and this is definitely one of them. Herod the Great was King of Judea at the time of Jesus' birth, and historians agree that he had a very cruel streak. He executed three of his own sons, as well as his wife and multiple members of her family! It's not surprising that such a ruthless man would order the murder of all the baby boys in Bethlehem when he felt that one of them threatened his power.

Jesus the refugee

We've already learned that Jesus was born into a poor peasant family, to unmarried teenagers. Now we find out that his family had to escape King Herod's violence by fleeing to another country, and that they were never able to return to their home out of fear of being killed. The eternal and glorious Lord of Creation came to earth and humbly joined a poor refugee family!

Throughout all four Gospels there's a clear pattern: Jesus always identifies himself with the people who are outsiders. He always draws near to the people hurting most. He always stands with the powerless. He says in Matthew 25 that however we treat the poorest, weakest, most disadvantaged people around us is how we're treating him personally. In his very first sermon in Luke 4, he introduced his entire public ministry with these powerful words from Isaiah 61:

The Escape to Egypt

"The Spirit of the Lord is on me,
because he has anointed me
to proclaim good news to the poor.
He has sent me to proclaim freedom for the prisoners
and recovery of sight for the blind,
to set the oppressed free,
to proclaim the year of the Lord's favour."

It shouldn't surprise us that our God cares so deeply for the weak and the hurting — this is who he's always been! The whole way through the Old Testament, God shows some of his harshest anger towards his people when they don't look after the most powerless people in their communities: widows, orphans, the poor, and sojourners (people from other places).

Take a look at Isaiah 58 as one example. There, we see that God was disgusted by Israelites (which was the original name for Jewish people) who acted religious one day a week but then took advantage of vulnerable people on all the other days. He was furious at their society for being so corrupt that rich people were treated better than poor people. He hated it when his people ignored the urgent needs of their neighbors and didn't provide any practical help for them. God pretty much says, "Why would I listen to your prayers if you live like that?"

For those of you among the millions of refugees in the world today who have had to leave your homes and loved ones behind, I hope it's a beautiful encouragement that the Son of God identifies with you. For those of you who are poor or oppressed today, know that he personally understands your suffering. But for those of us who are privileged enough to live in safety and security, we should be asking ourselves some challenging questions: do I treat the poor people around me with the same love and respect as I would show to Jesus himself? Do I care for the people society rejects with the same compassion and boldness as God does? Do I share God's holy anger at the abuse of vulnerable people in my community? Am I actively working to make my local area a more loving, just place for all people?

Prophecies fulfilled

You may have already noticed that Matthew regularly talks about Old Testament prophecies that are being fulfilled by the life of Jesus. In today's reading alone it is mentioned three times. So why is this such a big deal?

Don't forget that the original audience reading these words were Christians who had grown up Jewish. The Jewish Scriptures are what we call the Old Testament, so Matthew's readers knew the Old Testament prophecies very well. For many generations Jewish people had been expecting a Messiah to come as the savior of their people, to lead them to peace and to be their king. Hundreds of prophecies about the coming Messiah are included all through the Old Testament, written many hundreds of years before Jesus' birth! Matthew includes so many references to these prophecies in order to prove to his earliest readers that Jesus was exactly who he said he was: the Savior of the world. In fact, at one point Jesus even explains to some of his disciples how all of the prophecies in the Old Testament are about him (Luke 24:27).

So why did many Jewish people still struggle to believe Jesus was the Messiah? They were hoping for a savior who would defeat their Roman rulers in a mighty battle, and who would build a new kingdom of peace and prosperity for them. They expected a strong warrior, a royal king, or a powerful leader. As we've already seen, right from the day he was born Jesus didn't exactly fit the picture they had in their heads. As we continue studying Matthew's Gospel together, put yourself in their shoes, and honestly ask: would you have believed that Jesus was the Son of God?

Reflect and respond

1. *It's pretty amazing that the Creator of the universe would choose to make his Son's earthly family poor, homeless refugees. What does this choice show you about the things God cares about?*
2. *Think about the people who might feel like outsiders in your community, or who are disrespected or mistreated by others, or who just don't fit in. How might it change your perspective to imagine Jesus as one of them? How might it change the way you treat them?*

The Escape to Egypt

Heavenly Father,
Thank you that when your Son became human he wasn't just some rich prince with a perfect life.
He was normal, and poor, and he went through very hard things.
Thank you that he knows what it feels like to be lonely and lost.
Show me ways that I can help make my community a more just, loving place, in a way that honors you and pleases your heart.
Help me to love others the way that you love me.

In Jesus' name,
Amen

Meditation verse for the day:

Is not this the kind of fasting I have chosen:
to loose the chains of injustice and untie
the cords of the yoke, to set the oppressed free
and break every yoke?
(Isaiah 58:6)

Day 5

John the Baptist — Part 1

(Read Matthew 3:1–6)

In this chapter we meet John the Baptist, an oddly dressed guy who lived a simple life in the desert. John was passionate about just one thing: preparing God's people for the coming of the Messiah. We know from the Gospel of Luke that John and Jesus were distant relatives, but we aren't told if they actually knew each other before this. What John did know is that a Messiah would be coming. He knew the Old Testament prophecies, and took them very seriously. So how was he encouraging other Jewish people to get themselves prepared for the Savior's arrival? Two steps: confessing their sins and being baptized to show their repentance. Today we'll just look at the first of these steps, and tomorrow we'll examine the second.

When we confess to something, it means we own up to it, and we admit what we've done wrong. But what exactly is it that we've done wrong?

An uncomfortable topic

These days lots of people find it awkward to talk about sin, because they don't want to come across as judgemental or old-fashioned. Others misinterpret the Bible as saying we should hate ourselves and go through life feeling ashamed of who we are. Tragically, even some churches and Christian leaders talk about sin in a way that's spiritually abusive and controlling, which only leads to people feeling overwhelmed by guilt.

Many people are also really offended by the idea that we're all sinful. The world tells us there's no such thing as right and wrong, and all that matters is what we want and think and feel. Our super-individualistic culture encourages us to follow wherever our hearts lead us, no matter what anyone else thinks. We reject the idea that someone else has the right to tell us what's best for us. We're told we should be able to do whatever makes us happy.

If you find the idea of sin to be uncomfortable or offensive, think about it this way: if you bought an expensive new phone, wouldn't you want to know how to use it properly? Now let's be honest, you might not read the whole instruction manual, but you would at least want to know how to turn it on, and what special features it has. You would want to find out what's going to break it, and how you can stop it getting damaged. One way of thinking about the Bible is as the instruction manual for human beings. God designed and created us. He knows us better than we know ourselves! He also loves us and wants us to live happy lives in healthy relationships with him and the people around us. The Bible tells us how to live that life. It tells us what's good for us. It also warns us about what's bad for us. But in his love for us, God will never force us to obey him. He allows us the freedom to choose his way or to try and live our own way, even though he knows that will only lead us into pain and hurt. He gives us the Bible to teach us how to find the joy and satisfaction we were designed to experience, through right relationships with him and with each other.

A complex topic

The Bible says we're all sinners. But what exactly is sin? There are lots of slightly different definitions out there, but throughout the Bible there's one theme that comes up over and over and over again, which helps us define sin very simply:

> *Sin is anything we think or say or do, that doesn't put God first.*

Romans 1:18–32 explains that if we don't put God first we aren't honoring him for who he us, which is the worst thing we can ever do. Not treating God as God is the root cause of every other sin. So sin isn't just bad things like murder or stealing or lying. Sin is also doing good things for the wrong reasons. For example, we can help little old ladies cross the street all day every day, but if we're only doing it to make ourselves feel good then we're still sinning because we're putting ourselves first, not God. Sin is also loving wonderful things like our families or possessions more than we love God. God gives us so many beautiful gifts to enjoy in this life, but if we treasure the gifts more than we treasure the Giver, it's a sin. God has to come first. He should be at the center of everything we think or say or do. Sin is living life in a way that pushes God to the side, not giving him the respect and adoration and praise he rightly deserves.

You might think that God's a bit self-absorbed to command us to put him first in every single part of our lives. A human who expected that from us would be considered dangerously ego-centric. But the Bible is also a lot more than just an instruction manual for life; it's God's own story of who he is. That's actually its main purpose. The Bible is how God has chosen to teach us about himself. And as we read the Bible, we learn that God is not just our loving Father and Creator, he is also awe-inspiringly glorious, perfectly holy, and sacred beyond our wildest dreams. He's so powerful, and so wise, and so good, that our little minds have no way of fully comprehending him. He's completely set apart from us in every way. The more we get to know him through the Bible, the more we can clearly see that he absolutely deserves to be first in our lives. He deserves to be more important to us than anything or anyone else. He deserves all the praise we could ever give him. In fact, he deserves more honor and love than we could ever offer in a million lifetimes. So God actually has every right to command us to put him first. Nothing less makes any logical sense. It's literally what we were made for. And so it's also where we'll find more joy and satisfaction than we could ever dream of!

Repenting for our sin

Now that we've looked at what sin actually is, let's talk about what John the Baptist was telling people to do: confessing and repenting for sin. Repenting means being deeply sorry for living a life that rejects and dishonors God. Repentance isn't just empty words we repeat every time we mess up as a sort of Get Out of Jail Free card. Our forgiveness doesn't depend on whether or not we remember to list ever sin we've ever done. When we confess to God and repent, we're turning our hearts away from our sin. We're saying we hate our sin. We're asking God to forgive us and free us from the power of our sin. We're saying to God that we know we can't be righteous on our own; we need him to rescue us. (To be righteous means to be right with God, to have no guilt before him, and to owe him no debt.)

Reflect and respond

1. *How does it make you feel to be told that you're a sinner in desperate need of God's forgiveness? Why do you think it makes you feel that way?*
2. *Think about a sin you struggle with. How are you dishonoring God with that sin?*
3. *What specific sin do you need to repent of today?*

Lord God Almighty,
You are majestic and glorious, powerful and holy, mighty and merciful, perfect and loving, wise and good!
Thank you that you have invited me to have a personal relationship with you, even though I've done nothing to deserve it.
Lord, I repent of my sin.
I'm sorry for trying to be the lord of my own life.
I'm sorry for dishonoring you with my thoughts and words and actions.
Please show me the parts of my life where there's sin I need to confess to you.
Thank you for your forgiveness and mercy and grace.

In Jesus' name,
Amen

Meditation verse for the day:

All have sinned and fall short of the glory of God.
(Romans 3:23)

Day 6

John the Baptist — Part 2
(Read Matthew Chapter 3)

Yesterday we learned that John the Baptist was encouraging the local Jewish people to prepare their hearts and lives for the coming Messiah. Today let's focus on the second step of that preparation process: baptism.

If you've been around Christians long enough, you might know that baptism can be a controversial topic. For today, let's not get into the controversies and just focus on what the Bible says about the meaning of baptism.

A public symbol

Baptism involves using water to symbolically show that a person is now a follower of Jesus. Some churches sprinkle water over the person's head, and others dunk the person completely underwater. However it's done, baptism isn't some magical ritual that literally washes away people's sin with water. Christians get baptized as a public action to represent what's privately happened in our hearts. Does that mean that after being baptized we'll never sin again? Of course not – we're still human. Does it mean that we need to be re-baptized every time we repent for our sin? Thankfully not, or we'd all be getting baptized again every day.

Sometimes people get it a little backwards and think that baptism is what makes you a Christian. Not quite! Think about it like marriage. Just because someone puts a wedding ring on their finger, it doesn't mean they are automatically married, right? To be married, they have to make a serious commitment to another person in front of their friends and family (or at least a couple of witnesses), and then sign some legal documents. The rings are just an external symbol of that heart commitment. In the same way, baptism is an outward sign to tell the world about an inward spiritual change that's already happened inside us.

The inward spiritual change

So what exactly is this spiritual change that baptism symbolizes? In Romans 6 and Colossians 2 we learn that baptism is a metaphor for the spiritual death and new life we have in Christ. Going into the baptism water represents dying and being buried, and coming up out of the water – washed and clean – represents our new spiritual birth. Using death as a metaphor sounds pretty extreme, but it's trying to get across the idea that when we become Christians, we die to who we used to be and become a brand new creation. We die to sin so that we can become alive to God through Jesus. We're completely leaving behind our old ways of trying to do life on our own terms. We're no longer who we once were. We're starting a brand new life in a right relationship with God.

Reflect and respond

1. *If you have been baptized, what did your baptism symbolize to you? If you haven't been baptized yet, what does today's passage make you think about getting baptized in the future?*

2. *How does thinking about the brand new life you have in Jesus encourage you?*

Father,
Thank you that you love me so much that you made a way to bring me back into a right relationship with you.
Thank you for the completely new life that you've given me as your child.
Thank you for the powerful symbol of baptism, as a way for me to show the world what you've done deep in my heart.
I love you.

In Jesus' name,
Amen

Meditation verse for the day:

Repent and be baptized, every one of you,
in the name of Jesus Christ for the forgiveness
of your sins. And you will receive the gift
of the Holy Spirit.
(Acts 2:38)

Day 7

Jesus in the Wilderness

(Read Matthew 4:1–11)

Be prepared for spiritual attack!

Up until this point in his life, Jesus had been a carpenter in a small country town. His baptism by John signalled the beginning of his public ministry, when he started doing miracles and making his identity as the Son of God known in the community. It's not a coincidence that this is also the time where he comes under serious spiritual attack! The devil was probably willing to try anything to stop Jesus from fulfilling his mission as Savior of the world.

1 Peter 5:8 describes the devil as a hungry lion, prowling around looking for ways to destroy us. The Bible also frequently describes life on this earth as a war between the spiritual forces of good and evil. We have to be ready to fight for what we believe in, and to stand up for our relationship with God at any cost. You might even find that the closer you're walking with God, and the more you're sharing the hope of Jesus with the people around you, the more spiritual attack you experience! That makes sense: Satan is going to put extra effort into trying to destroy anyone who's a threat to him. We should always be prepared for his attempts to drag us down.

What does spiritual warfare look like?

Take a closer look at the things the devil is trying to tempt Jesus with: food, physical safety, and power. None of those are necessarily bad things. Satan is cunning, and doesn't always attack our faith in obvious ways. He wants us to relax and forget that there's a war going on, so that we lower our guard.

Sometimes he tempts us with fun distractions like social media or sport or a new romance. These distractions can consume our thoughts and energy until we have no time left for God. Sometimes the devil tempts us with good things like success at school or work, or love and approval from others. Many of us are tempted away from our faith in Jesus simply by Satan's promise of a happy life. We slowly drift into a comfortable, worldly lifestyle that revolves purely around our own pleasures and desires and barely even realize that we don't have a personal relationship with God anymore. The list of ways Satan attacks Christians is never-ending. Depression and anxiety. Ambition. Greed. Loneliness. Jealousy. Entertainment. Power. Partying. Addiction. Insecurity. Fear. Busy lives.

Are you ready to fight against him when he attacks you? Or are you just floating defenceless through life, ignoring that there's a cosmic war waging over your soul?

Know who you are and whose you are

We get a really interesting insight into the devil's warfare tactics from this passage. We read in Matthew 3 that when Jesus was baptized, God spoke from heaven and said, "This is my Son, whom I love; with him I am well pleased." It was straight after this that Jesus headed into the desert for forty days and was tempted by Satan.

Now look again at verses 3 and 6 at the exact words the devil uses, not once, but twice: "If you are the Son of God . . . " What's his strategy here? Why is he using this language? He's trying to take the truth that God has just declared over Jesus and sow seeds of doubt in Jesus' mind. He is trying to question Jesus' identity, right after God has publicly announced who Jesus is. It is the same sneaky approach he took in the garden of Eden when he tempted Eve to eat the forbidden fruit, by saying to her, "Did God really say . . . ?" (Genesis 3:1).

This is still one of the devil's most effective weapons against us today. He wants to put doubts into your heart about your identity in God's eyes. He wants you to question God's goodness and the wisdom of his plan for your life. He wants you to feel uncertain about whether you're really a beloved child of God. He wants you to doubt if you can actually trust everything God says in the Bible. He wants you to wonder if you have a better chance of finding happiness by following the world's way instead of God's way.

Being ready to fight back against this kind of attack takes daily work. To fight the lies of Satan, we have to be prepared with the Truth. We have to know who God is, and who God says we are. We have to know by heart what the Bible says about our identity as children of a loving Father, which never changes no matter how we feel or what the devil tells us. We strengthen ourselves for battle by abiding in God's Word, and letting it dwell inside us in a real and deep way. This means knowing and loving the Bible! Soaking our minds in it all through the day, day after day, week after week, year after year. Meditating on it, and singing it out, and thinking carefully about it, and studying it, and exploring it passionately. Asking the Holy Spirit to help us really understand it. Talking regularly to faithful friends and church leaders about it. Letting it shape us from the inside out. Not because the Bible is some kind of magic book, but because the Bible is where we meet God.

If we truly understand and trust the message of the gospel then we'll be better prepared to fight the devil's spiritual attacks. That doesn't mean it'll be easy or that we'll feel like we're winning all the time. But it means we will have our weapons available at any moment, ready to fight.

We all have moments where we doubt God and aren't sure what we really believe. You aren't alone if you feel that way right now. Even Thomas, one of Jesus' own disciples, doubted that Jesus had actually been raised from the dead. But be encouraged. Jesus wasn't angry at Thomas for doubting, instead he kindly showed himself to Thomas in just the way he needed, to help him stop doubting and believe (John 20:24–28). If you're doubting who God is today, pray. Pray for God to personally show you who he is. Ask him to reveal himself to you in just the way you need. Pray that he'll strengthen your faith and help you trust him. And then open up your Bible and wait to hear from him, expecting him to answer through his Word.

Reflect and respond

1. What sort of temptations or doubts is Satan attacking your faith with?
2. How can you abide in God's Word more this week, to prepare yourself to fight against the devil's attacks?

Loving God,
It's so encouraging that Jesus knows what it feels like to be tempted.
Thank you that he can personally relate to the struggles I go through when the devil attacks my faith and tries to make me question you.
Help me to be better prepared for spiritual warfare.
Give me the motivation and self-discipline to spend quality time reading the Bible every day, hiding it away in my heart so that it's inside me when I need it most.
Teach me how to really understand the Bible, please Holy Spirit.
Deepen my faith in you so I can stand confidently against the lies of the enemy.

In Jesus' name,
Amen

Meditation verse for the day:

Do not be afraid of them;
the Lord your God himself will fight for you.
(Deuteronomy 3:22)

Day 8

Jesus Calls His Disciples

(Read Matthew 4:12–25)

These days the word 'disciple' isn't very common, but in the Bible it refers to someone who's a student of Jesus. These people literally follow Jesus around, listening to everything he says and learning from him. In this passage Jesus calls his first four disciples, who were all fishermen.

Leave and follow

The two things Jesus asks of these four fishermen are things that Jesus asks of all of us: to leave behind the life we're currently living and follow him wherever he leads. That's not a small decision to make! And take a close look at their amazing responses: "At once they left their nets", and "immediately they left the boat and their father" (verses 20 and 22). At once! Immediately! They dropped *everything* the instant Jesus invited them to be his disciples.

Now if I'm being honest, I don't think I would have had as much faith as those fishermen. I would have overthought it and hesitated and procrastinated. I would have asked Jesus a bunch of questions, like: When will I see my parents and friends again? I'm an introvert, so can I get weekends off for some alone-time? Where exactly will I be following you to? Will it be really hard? Once Jesus had given me enough information about what I was committing to, I might have considered leaving my old life behind and becoming his disciple. Maybe.

Becoming a Christian requires trusting God, and stepping out in faith. We trust that God is good and that he loves us. We trust that he knows what he's doing, and that he only wants the best for us. But we never know exactly where following Jesus will take us in life, or what we'll be asked to give up for him. One of the greatest chapters in the Bible is Hebrews 11, which lists dozens of Bible heroes and explains that their incredible stories all started with a step of faith. And then another step of faith. Step after step after step of faith. And God used each of them in wonderful, unique, special ways. None of us get told in advance what our earthly story will look like when we choose to become a disciple of Jesus. But we're promised that God will never leave our side. We're promised that he is for us, and that he loves us, and that he's a treasure worth everything we have and much more.

There are many people around the world who become Christians knowing that it'll mean their families will reject them for ever. Some are even killed by their communities, or thrown in jail and tortured. Others follow Jesus onto the mission field, where they leave behind their friends and family and home, all for the chance to tell others about God's love for them. God leads some people to change all the friends they hang out with, or to give all their money away, or to stay single for their whole life.

Following Jesus is simple, but it is not easy. Let me repeat that: following Jesus is simple, but it's not easy. What I mean is, there aren't lots of complicated steps to being a Christian, but it always comes at a high cost. We're all called to leave things behind. We're all called to die to ourselves and our selfish desires. We're all called to step out in faith. Do you trust God enough to give up whatever he asks? Is it worth it to you, to get to be in a relationship with him?

Fishers of people

It's also important to see here that Jesus doesn't invite the fishermen to become his disciples just so they can be his friends and learn lots of interesting things from him and live happily ever after. He wants to train them up to actually do something: go out and fish for people (verse 19). That metaphorical language might seem like Jesus is making a bit of a dad joke (they're fishermen, remember!) and maybe he is. But his point is that their new purpose will be to go out into the world and teach other people how to follow Jesus too.

Jesus Calls His Disciples

As Christians, our responsibility is not to go to church every Sunday and enjoy a comfortable life of private faith in God. We're meant to lovingly share the hope and the joy that we have with others. Our job is to spread the good news, teaching others just as we've been taught. We're being called to *be* disciples of Jesus and also to *make* disciples of Jesus!

The example I've heard is this: imagine that you've discovered the cure for cancer. Wouldn't you want to tell the whole world about it? To share the cure far and wide? To save as many people as you can from dying unnecessarily? As Christians, we have The Cure. His name is Jesus. He's the only cure for our slavery to sin, the cure to our separation from God, and the cure to our loneliness, our selfishness, our hopelessness, and our shame. He's everything we need and more. He's everything we've ever wanted. Why on earth wouldn't we want to share that good news with everyone, so they can find their cure in Jesus too?

Reflect and respond

1. *Deep down, do you really believe that having a relationship with God is worth whatever it might cost you? Why or why not?*
2. *What things in life would you struggle most to give up for God if he asked? Is there anything you would absolutely refuse to give up for him? Take some time to pray about these things, because they're probably idols in your heart.*

Almighty God,
It's such a privilege that you invite me to be your disciple.
It's such grace that you offer to walk with me through life; to teach me, to encourage me, and to change me from the inside out.
I don't deserve your friendship or your love.
Please show me your trustworthiness and help me trust you more.
Please forgive me for not taking every opportunity to share your love with the people around me.
Help me to value you more than I value what other people think of me.

In Jesus' name,
Amen

Meditation verse for the day:

Jesus called them, and immediately
they left the boat and their father
and followed him.
(Matthew 4:21–22)

Day 9

The Beatitudes — Part 1

(Read Matthew 5:1–12)

The Sermon on the Mount is the longest of Jesus' recorded sermons, and this particular part of it is very well-known as the beatitudes. The word *beatitude* comes from a Latin word meaning 'blessedness' or 'happiness.' Pastor Jon Tyson explains that the beatitudes are like the official core values and priorities and promises of Jesus' kingdom. "Jesus is saying, 'I'm the King, and I'm bringing you a kingdom, and now I want to show you the characteristics of what happens when people align with my rule and reign.'"[1]

The first thing you might notice about this list of blessings is that the people he's talking about don't sound very appealing. Mourners? Meek? Persecuted? These are not the type of people we usually dream of being. This list would have seemed just as odd – and maybe even shocking – to Jesus' original audience. If we were writing our own beatitudes for the world today, who would we say is blessed or happy?

Happy are people who are rich and attractive, for they shall be admired by others.

Happy are those who have found the love of their life, for they are living the good life.

Happy are the hard-working, for they shall have successful careers.

---

1. Tyson, "Flourishing in the Kingdom", 1:02:11.

Happy are they with the most social media followers, for they shall be famous.

But this is not God's way. Remember how he chose poor unmarried teenagers to be Jesus' earthly parents? Remember how he decided to include outsiders and prostitutes and murderers and abuse survivors in his family tree? Once again, Jesus is showing us that God's way of looking at the world is opposite to what we would expect. The kingdom of heaven is upside down and inside out. The things God values are completely different to the things the world values.

Blessed are the poor in spirit

What does it mean to be poor in spirit? Another way of phrasing it might be to say blessed are the humble. A person with biblical humility is self-aware enough to see that they are sinful and broken, and that they can't be their own savior.

Don't get this confused with having poor self-esteem or being depressed. Christian humility is not at all about hating ourselves or living with an overwhelming sense of guilt. Humility means we have a correct view of who we are compared with who God is. It means we understand how majestic and powerful and righteous and perfect God is, and can see clearly that we don't come anywhere close to him in any way. He's completely set apart from us. He exists on a whole different level than we can even dream of. Humble people are simply aware of their own unworthiness in the face of God's perfect holiness.

Blessed are those who mourn

There's more than one application of this blessing. One way of reading it is that Jesus is offering encouragement to people who experience loss and deep sadness in this life, and promising them future comfort in heaven. Throughout the Bible God says that he'll be a refuge for us in the hardest times, and that in heaven he'll wipe all of the tears from our eyes and we'll never need to cry again. In Isaiah 66:13 he even says he'll comfort us the way a loving mother comforts her crying baby. This beatitude is an encouragement to anyone who has grieved, anyone who has experienced deep injustice, or anyone who feels hopelessness and despair in life.

Another way of understanding this blessing is to recognize that it's linked to the first beatitude, and that Jesus is talking about people who are humbly mourning how sinful they are. Genuine repentance doesn't mean you only feel sorry for your sin once you get caught. True repentance means feeling broken-hearted that you hurt God, and disgusted by your sin. It means genuinely hating what you did, and being sad that you dishonored God. This is also a type of mourning that will finally be over in heaven, where we won't struggle against our sins anymore.

Blessed are the meek

Meekness is similar to humility or gentleness. People often think that being meek means you're a pushover, or that you're very quiet and shy. But let's explore how meekness is defined in the Bible.

James 1:19 connects meekness with being "quick to listen, slow to speak, and slow to become angry". Next, James encourages Christians to meekly listen to and learn from the Bible. This shows us that being meek also means to be teachable, to accept instruction from the Holy Spirit, and not to become defensive when our weaknesses are pointed out. And then James 3 explains that true wisdom leads to meekness. He says that meek people are not selfish, boastful, or envious, but instead are gentle, caring peacemakers.

Blessed are those who hunger and thirst for righteousness

Have you ever been extremely hungry? Or incredibly thirsty? In that situation, your hunger or thirst becomes all you can think about, and you would do almost anything to get your hands on some food or drink. This is the kind of passion and deep desire that Jesus is talking about here.

But what does it mean to be passionate about righteousness? The righteousness of God is his holiness and his perfection. If we're hungering for righteousness it means that every single day we long to personally experience more of God's majesty and glory. We're desperately yearning to become more like Jesus. We would give anything to be right with God, to be at peace with him, to honor him properly.

And the most stunning part of this beatitude? God promises that if we hunger and thirst for righteousness he will fill us right up. He will give us more of himself. He will make us more like Jesus. He will satisfy our spiritual hunger for something more.

Reflect and respond

1. Which of these beatitudes do you find most encouraging, and why?
2. Which of these beatitudes do you find most challenging, and why?

Oh Lord,
You offer the kingdom of heaven to those who cry out to you in humility.
You lovingly comfort those who mourn.
You give the earth to those who humbly treasure your wisdom.
You fill up those who hunger and thirst for your righteousness.
You are so kind.
I worship you, oh Lord!

In Jesus' name,
Amen

Meditation verse for the day:

Blessed are those who hunger and thirst for righteousness,
for they will be filled.
(Matthew 5:6)

Day 10

The Beatitudes — Part 2

(Read Matthew 5:1–12)

Today we're going to look at the second half of Jesus' counter-cultural beatitudes. 'Counter-cultural' means doing something different from what's normal to other people. Are you already getting the picture that Jesus is a pretty counter-cultural guy?

Blessed are the merciful

What is mercy? In Jesus' famous story of the Good Samaritan in Luke 10, he says mercy means having compassion on the people around us, and caring practically for them in whatever ways we can. The Bible describes God as being rich in mercy towards us. His mercy means that he forgives our sins and doesn't stay angry with us, even though we definitely deserve his punishment. In his beautiful book *Truth on Fire*, pastor Adam Ramsey says that God's mercy is shown by his tenderness towards us, and the "life-restoring gentleness"[1] he treats us with, even on our worst days. Isn't that such a wonderful description of God's mercy? When we least deserve it, he's tender and gentle with us in a way that breathes life back into us, rebuilding us and restoring us and renewing us and refreshing us.

But what does it actually look like to be merciful?

Does it mean we let others walk all over us?

---

1. Ramsey, *Truth on Fire*, 122.

Does it mean we don't report criminals and just let them get away with their crimes?

Should we stay in abusive relationships?

Absolutely not.

Throughout the Bible, God is described as a God of mercy *and* justice. He holds all humans accountable for our choices. There are consequences for our actions. Both mercy and justice are central to the nature or God, and we should be passionate about both things too. This means that when people treat us badly, we can forgive them and be kind to them, without continuing to let them take advantage of us. It means we can leave unhealthy or dangerous relationships while also praying that our abuser gets the help they need for their own healing.

I recently read about an inspiring and heart-wrenching example of Christian mercy. An older Christian couple's only son was murdered. Justice was served, and the murderer was sent to jail for a long time. But then the older couple started writing letters to him. They started visiting him in prison. Instead of hatred, they offered him forgiveness. Instead of heaping shame on his head for what he'd done, they generously welcomed him into their family. They treated him as a son. They showed compassion to him a way that he definitely did not deserve. Now *that* is radical mercy. That is mercy just like God has shown us. It's mercy that probably cost that older couple a lot of tears and heartache, but they chose to do it anyway.

Blessed are the pure in heart

In verse 8, Jesus says that in his kingdom the pure in heart are blessed. Your friends and family might think they know you well, but only God can see your heart. Only God knows all of your deepest, darkest thoughts and feelings and desires. That's a pretty embarrassing and humbling thought, right? There's some nasty stuff in there! The good news is that he knows it all and still loves you with his whole heart!

Jesus doesn't want to just change the way Christians behave; he wants to transform our hearts so that they're clean and pure and holy. So what does it actually mean to be pure in heart? To be honest and truthful. To say what we mean, and do what we say, instead of being a hypocrite. To love God with our whole heart, not just part of it.

And when we're pure in heart, Jesus says we will see God. Seeing God doesn't mean getting to have a look at his face and seeing what he looks like;

it means feeling his presence, and getting to know him personally and intimately. Recognizing him for who he really is. What an amazing promise!

Blessed are the peacemakers

The whole Bible tells the story of God making peace with us, his beloved children. We've run away from him, we've fought against him, we've ruined his beautiful creation and tried to do life our own way. Instead of just abandoning us to our own terrible choices, he chases after us, forgives us, pays our debts for us, and welcomes us back into his family with open arms. He's the ultimate peacemaker.

As his children, we should also be peacemakers. Once again, this doesn't mean we just ignore the bad things other people do and pretend they doesn't exist. A wise friend of mine calls that "peace-faking": pretending there is peace when there really isn't. Sometimes real peace-making means we first have to dig up deeply hidden hurts and expose them to the light so that we can deal with them in a healthy way. It might be hard or uncomfortable or awkward.

Being peace-makers means that we always try to work towards repairing broken relationships, building bridges with our enemies, and bringing about reconciliation and harmony. That's not an easy thing to do. It'll probably cost us something personally, just like making peace with us cost Jesus more than we could ever know. And we might not always succeed at making peace. But we should deeply desire it and work for it every chance we get.

Blessed are those who are persecuted because of righteousness

Persecution means different things in different places. Tens of thousands of Christians around the world are killed every year for their faith in Jesus. Many more Christians are kicked out of home, become refugees because their lives are in danger, or have to keep their faith a secret. Millions of Christians around the world meet in secret churches, or don't own their own copy of the Bible because it's illegal where they live.

Even if that's a long way from your own personal experience, the Bible does say that *everyone* who follows Jesus will face persecution of some kind. We should expect it and prepare for it. Maybe you'll lose friends because you choose not to live the same kind of lifestyle as them. Maybe people will spread false rumors about you and try to damage your reputation. Maybe people will laugh at your way of living and call you old-fashioned or narrow-minded or boring. Maybe you'll be left out and feel lonely and rejected.

Verse 12 tells us to "rejoice and be glad" when we experience persecution for being followers of Jesus. It's important to understand that we're not being told here to keep a smile on our face in spite of the pain inside, or to fake it till we make it. Jesus is telling us to genuinely change how we feel about it! Does that sound impossible to you? There are two clues in verse 12 about how we can actually do that. Firstly, we need to keep our focus on heaven. We were made for more than this broken, hurting world. This earth isn't our home, and this isn't the place where we'll ever feel completely comfortable. When we keep our minds and hearts focused on heaven and the joy and fulfilment that we're going to have there, we can see any struggles that we have here on earth from a different perspective. Secondly, Jesus reminds us that all of the great prophets in the Bible were persecuted. We are in good company! We can read their stories to encourage and inspire us to stand firm. Remember that you're not alone in this spiritual battle.

Reflect and respond

1. *The beatitudes show us that our God values very different things than the world does. Can people see that your faith causes you to live differently to everyone else around you? Why or why not?*
2. *Think of a person you have a difficult relationship with. How can you honor God by being a peacemaker in that relationship?*

Father God,
You are the God of mercy.
Please teach me to show mercy to others.
You are the God of purity.
Please give me a clean, pure heart that's all for you.
You are the God who pursues us to make peace with us.
Please help me be a peacemaker.
You are the God of all comfort, a refuge for us in the storm.
Thank you that I can have your peace and joy and hope even if the world hates me. Thank you that I have a home in your kingdom.

The Beatitudes — Part 2

Help me live a counter-cultural life that shows other people how great you are.
I just want to bring you glory.

In Jesus' name,
Amen

Meditation verse for the day:

Be merciful, just as your Father is merciful.
(Luke 6:36)

Day 11

Righteousness

(Read Matthew 5:13–48)

This passage includes some of Jesus' most famous teachings on how to live a righteous life. It would have been quite shocking for his original audience! We should be challenged by it as well.

Salt and light

As we've been reading in the beatitudes, Christians shouldn't live lives that look exactly the same as everyone else. If we belong to God's upside-down kingdom, we should be growing more and more humble, meek, merciful, and pure-hearted. We should be peacemakers whose main desire is to experience more of God every day. We shouldn't be idolizing money or fame or power, we should be pursuing righteousness. We shouldn't be selfishly doing only what benefits us in life, we should be following wherever Jesus leads us, no matter what we have to leave behind.

Verses 13 to 16 remind us that as Christians we're not called to a relationship with Jesus simply to have a nice, comfortable, private faith that no one else knows about. We're meant to be public about it. Our faith should be obvious to others. We're like salt in food; we bring the flavor! We're like a town perched right on the top of a hill; we can be seen for miles around! We're like a lamp in a room; we brighten up every corner of the darkness! And why is it important that we're public about our faith? Not for our own reputation, but so that the people around us will see God at work in us and see that he's worthy of their worship too.

The fulfilment of the law

Remember that Jesus was Jewish, and that in his lifetime the New Testament hadn't been written yet. When he talks about the Law and the Prophets in verse 17, it's what we now call the Old Testament. Jesus is making a huge, controversial statement here to his Jewish audience about who he is. He is claiming to be the fulfilment of the entire Old Testament!

He says he's the one all the prophesies are about, and the one all the metaphors and symbols refer to. He's what the whole story has been about from beginning to end. But in verse 18 he says we can't just throw away the Old Testament as if it's over and done with. This should be a great encouragement to us to read the Old Testament for ourselves. It might seem confusing at first, but with the help of the Holy Spirit and faithful Christian teachers, the Old Testament is rich and beautiful and will help us more fully appreciate who Jesus is.

Jesus then makes a statement in verse 20 that's pretty harsh. He says unless we're even more righteous than the Pharisees, we won't be welcome in heaven. What he's saying is that being a Christian is a lot more than following rules. Jesus is interested in the righteousness of our hearts, not just how we act. The Pharisees were experts at behaving righteously and following the letter of the law perfectly, but Jesus says that what's happening inside us is much more important to him. He wants to be the center of our loves and desires and thoughts and feelings and deepest beliefs! He isn't honored by people who do all the right things but still carry around pride or selfishness or hatred in their spirits.

You have heard it was said

Next in our passage we have six different examples Jesus gives of Old Testament laws. Jesus takes each of these holy laws, given to the Israelites by God, and then changes them by saying, "But I tell you . . . " He overrides the existing laws from the Old Testament, making them even harder to follow. He makes the standard for righteousness even higher! He makes it even more impossible to follow these laws perfectly as a way of getting into heaven! Most of us can get through life without murdering anyone, but we get angry at other people all the time. Lots of us won't commit adultery (which is sexual activity outside of a marriage relationship), but we all look at someone else with lust in our hearts, maybe even dozens of times in a single day.

Jesus is showing us a few very important things here:

1. *He is equal to God.* God the Father set the laws for righteous living in the Old Testament, and God the Son has the authority and power to change them. Jesus and the Father are equals, and are one God.

2. *God is perfectly righteous.* These new, higher standards for righteousness are Jesus' way of showing us just how holy God really is. He is perfectly pure, perfectly holy, perfectly good. He is the only one who can ever meet these standards fully and be truly righteous.

3. *We can never measure up on our own.* Even if we try our hardest every day of our lives, we can never meet these new standards that Jesus is setting. We will never be righteous enough by ourselves. God is just too holy. And that's Jesus' whole point here! He wants us to realize how badly we need a Savior. He wants us to see that our only option is to humbly cry out to God for his mercy and grace. When we do this in faith, Jesus' righteousness is given to us as a free gift, and treated like it's our own. He takes our sin on himself and gives us his perfect righteousness in return. What a trade! As Christians, when we die and stand in front of God for judgment, he won't see any of our sinfulness. Jesus washed it away with his blood. All God will see is Jesus' perfect holiness, covering us from head to toe like a shining white robe. And because of Jesus' righteousness, he'll welcome us into heaven.

Reflect and respond

1. *Is your faith public or private? How could you be more like salt and light in the world, sharing your hope and joy with others?*

2. *How might your attitude towards reading and understanding the Old Testament change if you remember that it's actually all about Jesus?*

Righteousness

Lord,
Thank you for the whole Bible, not just the bits I find interesting and easy to understand.
Thank you that it's the story of who you are.
It's incredible to think that you chose to reveal yourself to us, so that we can get to know you personally.
Please forgive me for not treasuring your Word more.
Holy Spirit, please help me understand the parts that don't make sense to me.
Teach me how to see the glory and beauty of Jesus in every part of the Bible.
God, I want to know you more and more every day.
Show me your face.

In Jesus' name,
Amen

Meditation verse for the day:

Let your light shine before others,
that they may see your good deeds
and glorify your Father in heaven.
(Matthew 5:16)

Day 12

What's Going on in Your Heart?

(Read Matthew 6:1–18)

Once again, Jesus is reminding us that God cares far more about what's going on in our hearts than how we act. He warns us that just acting like 'good Christians' by donating to poor people, or praying lots, or fasting, is not going to impress him at all. He still wants us to do those things, because they're all important and good! But he wants us to do them out of love for him, not so that other people will admire us.

Boasting about ourselves online and bragging about our lives is so normal these days. We all know how easy social media makes it to show the world a version of ourselves that isn't real. We only post the best pictures and only show the things we want other people to know about. We hide away our insecurities and edit out our flaws as if they don't exist. Social media also preaches that if the world doesn't know about it, it might as well have never even happened. We post online about everything we do because we feel the need for people to know and comment on it. We want to be seen. We want to publicly admired.

In verse 3 Jesus tells us that we should keep our good deeds between us and God. This helps us be honest with ourselves about whether we're really doing it for God or for ourselves. Jesus uses the exaggerated picture of giving money to poor people with our right hand without even letting our left hand know about it. In our modern times, this might mean doing things like buying a homeless person lunch without ever telling anyone else you did it; or volunteering for a charity without ever posting about it online; or cleaning your grandma's house every week without the rest of your family finding out. If you literally can't handle doing good things without telling someone else about it, you might have a selfishness problem. You're probably not doing those things out of love for God, but out of love for yourself. You want the praise! You want the worship! You need to feed your pride! And Jesus says that's a huge problem.

As Christians, we should always be checking what's motivating our actions. Ask yourself: why are you doing good things? Why are you kind and generous to others? Why do you serve at church? Why do you pray the way you do when other people are listening? Do your social media posts glorify God, or glorify yourself?

The Lord's Prayer

Most of us spend a lot of our prayer time asking for things, right? Healing for this person, help with that thing, guidance for a particular decision, a miracle in that part of life. These are all good things to ask for, but we need to remember that God isn't Santa, and prayer is not just an opportunity to give him our wish-list.

If we only ever *ask* God for stuff when we pray, what does that tell him about our deepest feelings for him? It's obvious we only want a relationship with him because of what he can do *for* us, not because of who he is. Imagine if your best friend only ever talked to you when they needed money, or help with an assignment, or advice on their relationship problems. Imagine if they never came to chat simply because they enjoyed your company. Imagine if they never just wanted to let you know how much they appreciated you. Would you feel cared for, or would you feel used?

Jesus gives us some simple advice about how to pray. We don't have to use it every single time we pray, but it's a helpful guide. Let's break it down bit by bit:

- *Our Father in heaven:* Jesus starts by reminding us that God is our Father. Our loving dad. We're his beloved children! This is an intimate relationship with another person. But in the same breath, Jesus then reminds us that God is also in heaven, an eternal and powerful spirit beyond our wildest dreams. He is literally out of this world. He exists outside of time. He is so far beyond our imagination or understanding, but he still humbles himself to lovingly listen to us when we pray. Meditate on the beauty of that truth, and let it thrill your heart!

- *Hallowed be your name:* Hallowed means to be holy, honored, and admired. This line means, "God, I want you to get all the reverence and praise. You deserve it all! It's all about you." Jesus is showing us here that the main thing we should focus on when we pray is God. Not us, but him. We want him to be worshipped the way he deserves. We exist to praise him, and to show others how magnificent God is. This shouldn't just be the first thing we pray, it should also be the soundtrack of our entire lives.

- *Your kingdom come, your will be done, on earth as it is in heaven:* This is a huge, world-wide prayer with an eternal perspective. We're asking for God's holy, perfect, plan to be fulfilled around the world, as well as in our countries, communities, families, and individual hearts.

- *Give us today our daily bread:* Suddenly, this prayer changes. We're not focusing on huge, global things anymore; we're focusing on the tiny little everyday parts of human life, like food. God doesn't only care about the big stuff, he cares about *you*. He cares that you have what you need to get through the day ahead. He wants to provide for you to have a healthy body and mind and spirit. It's good to ask God for things we need! Just keep in mind that God sees the whole picture and knows what we actually need to get through the day ahead, not just what we think we need.

- *And forgive us our debts, as we also have forgiven our debtors:* We all sin, every day, over and over and over. We don't have to focus too much on our sin and let our guilt weigh us down, but we do need to humbly repent and ask for God's forgiveness. And because we know how much forgiveness we personally need every day, we should be ready to forgive people who sin against us, too. All of us need mercy!

- *Lead us not into temptation, but deliver us from the evil one:* God's forgiveness doesn't just mean we can happily keep on sinning every day, knowing we can always repent again tomorrow. When we really love God, we long to honor him with the way we live, so we ask him to help us to sin less and to protect us from Satan's attacks.

What's Going on in Your Heart?

Reflect and respond

1. *Who's being glorified by the good things you do? You or God? How can your life show off how great God is?*
2. *What key differences do you notice about the way you usually pray, and the way Jesus teaches us to pray? What do you leave out or include?*

Take some time now to slowly pray your way through the Lord's Prayer, adding your own personal details to each line.

Meditation verse for the day:

The Lord is near to all who call on him,
to all who call on him in truth.
(Psalm 145:18)

Day 13

Seek First His Kingdom and Righteousness

(Read Matthew 6:19–34)

Today's passage is all about experiencing more of God. Jesus is teaching us how to have a closer relationship with God, which will give us more security while we're alive on this earth, and more joy when we're in heaven for all eternity.

Where's your treasure stored?

Jesus warns us against having our treasure stored here on earth. Keep in mind he isn't referring to a literal treasure chest filled with gold and jewels, he's talking about the things our hearts love most. It might be fame and fortune, or it might be entertainment and fun activities. It might be food or cars or shopping or video games or our looks. Even family and friends, which are wonderful God-given blessings, shouldn't be the ultimate treasures of our hearts. Why not? Because they do not and cannot last forever. They can all be taken away from us in the blink of an eye. All it takes is one car accident, one sickness, one crime. We can't take them with us from our death bed into eternity. If our happiness and identity are dependent on things we might lose at any moment, we'll be very insecure, anxious people.

But what does it actually mean to store up our treasures in heaven? Jesus reminds us that God should be number one in our hearts. God should be our treasure. God's deep love for us should be the foundation of our identity and our security and our greatest joy. God's character should be our favourite thing to think about. Worshipping God should be our favourite thing to do. Heaven is where we'll spend all of eternity enjoying being with God, so even now our focus should be on him. Earthly things can be wonderful, but they can't come before God in our hearts.

Pastor Timothy Keller explains how we can discover what our idols are by taking a look at our imagination:

> "Archbishop William Temple once said, 'Your religion is what you do with your solitude.' In other words, the true god of your heart is what your thoughts effortlessly go to when there is nothing else demanding your attention. What do you enjoy daydreaming about? What occupies your mind when you have nothing else to think about? . . . What do you habitually think about to get joy and comfort in the privacy of your heart?"[1]

Solitude means your quiet time, your alone time. Those relaxed times where you're doing nothing but chilling and letting your mind wander. In those moments, what do you love to think about most often? Sports? Social media? A relationship? Your bank account? How many likes you got on social media? Keller and Temple are saying *that* thing is really your god. That thing is your treasure. That thing is what you're building your identity and sense of security on.

In verse 24 Jesus talks specifically about money. Compared with some other topics, Jesus actually talks quite regularly about money. Money itself is not evil, but it's a very popular idol in our society, and it was in Jesus' day as well. We all know that money can't buy happiness, but we often still act like it can. We make our important life choices around it, or base our sense of security on having enough of it. But Jesus makes it very clear here that loving money too much will get in the way of loving God.

Therefore, do not worry.

Verse 25 begins with the word 'therefore', which means 'because of this'. Whenever you see this word, you need to go back and read the verses that come before it for some context. It links two sections of Jesus' teaching, so it's important to read them together even though they are under separate headings in our Bibles.

---

1. Keller, *Counterfeit Gods*, 168.

This 'therefore' means Jesus is saying that *because* you're storing up your treasures in heaven instead of on earth, don't worry. *Because* God is your treasure, you don't have to be anxious about daily things. *Because* your identity and self-worth and security are safely stored in heaven, you don't need to fear the future. You can't lose God. If you're his child, he'll never let go of you. There's nothing you could do to make him love you any less, and nothing you could go through that will scare him away. There's nothing you will face that's too hard for him. He'll provide what you need to get through today (although it might look different to what you *think* you need.) Even death doesn't need to be scary anymore, because you'll be going home to spend eternity with him.

On the other hand, if my treasure is my bank account, I might worry when I lose my job. If my treasure is my family or friends, I might feel overwhelmed when someone I love gets a cancer diagnosis. If my treasure is my reputation, I might stress if someone says bad things about me. If my treasure is my appearance, I might get more anxious with every wrinkle or stretch mark. If my treasure is my physical abilities, I might get depressed when I experience an injury or disability. Can you see the freedom from worry that Jesus is offering us here? He's definitely not saying life will be perfect or easy, but he is saying we don't need to carry around the burden of worry. We can trust him to be everything we need.

This is particularly important for young people around the world today, because rates of anxiety and depression are higher than they've ever been before in history. Young people are struggling under the burden of worry in every area of life, and some are even taking their own lives because of it. Others try to escape the anxiety by distracting themselves every moment of every day. If worry is weighing you down today, take some time to re-read and meditate over Jesus' encouraging words in verses 25 – 33.

The answer

Jesus says the way to deal with our worry and anxiety is to store up our treasures in heaven. We already know that means to love him most, but verse 33 teaches us how to do that on a daily basis: by seeking first God's kingdom and his righteousness. Let's break down what that actually means:

- *Seek*. We have to be seeking, which is an active decision to look hard for something. Seeking is not just something that happens naturally or accidentally, it has to be a purposeful and deliberate choice. You have to plan for it. You have to make time for it. You have to prioritize it over other things. You have to have self-discipline to do it, and then keep on doing it day after day until you find what you're looking for.

- *First.* It has to be our first priority, the most important thing we do every day. We always find ways to make time for the things we love, even if it means waking up earlier or missing out on something else. Do you ever get to the end of a day or week or month and realize you were so busy you didn't spend any time with God? If that's happening regularly, then God is obviously not the first priority in your heart.
- *The kingdom of God.* When Jesus talks about the kingdom of God, he isn't talking about a literal, physical place on a map with a castle and a throne. He's talking about God's lordship and his reign as King.

So verse 33 says that what we're seeking to do every day as our first priority is make God the King over every part of our hearts and lives. We're submitting every part of who we are to him as our Lord. We're learning about his righteousness and asking him to make us holy like him. We're working to proclaim and announce his kingdom in the world around us. We're practicing trusting that he's sovereign. (Sovereign means there are no limits to his power. He has total control over absolutely everything.)

Do you struggle with anxiety or fear? Jesus offers hope for you today. Treasure God above any earthly thing, and trust him as the sovereign King over every situation in your life, and you'll find the secret to having unshakeable peace and joy.

Reflect and respond

1. *Think about the challenging quote from Timothy Keller. What do you usually daydream about? What's the first thing your mind goes to when you aren't busy or distracted? What do you enjoy thinking about most of all?*
2. *How will you make time to seek God's kingdom and righteousness first this week?*

Lord God and Heavenly Father,
I praise you because you are eternal and unchanging and sovereign.
You never fail and you will never let go of me.
I praise you that I can trust you to be everything I need, now and forevermore.
I repent for having treasures above you in my heart.
Please forgive me.
You deserve to be my first priority.
Thank you for the freedom you offer from stress and anxiety.
Fix my eyes and heart on you, Lord, and set me free from fear.
I want you to be the unshakeable foundation of my security and my identity and my joy.

In Jesus' name,
Amen

Meditation verse for the day:

Seek first his kingdom and his righteousness,
and all these things will be given to you as well.
(Matthew 6:33)

Day 14

A Warning and a Promise

(Read Matthew 7:1–12)

Even if you've read these words a hundred times before, there will always be new, life-changing glimpses of who God is in this passage. Take a moment to pray before you continue today's study, asking God's Spirit to help you learn more about his character, and to give you the humility and perspective to be able to see areas of your own life that aren't honoring him right now.

Judging others

We all hate the feeling of being judged. But it's part of our sinful human nature that we judge each other all the time. Even if we don't say a single word out loud, we judge others in our hearts all day long, from our closest friends to strangers on the street. In this passage, Jesus is giving a very strong warning to every single one of us about our dangerous tendency to be judgemental.

He says that we're hypocrites, judging other people more harshly than we judge ourselves. He accuses us of holding the people around us to a higher standard than we hold ourselves, and feeling so prideful and self-righteous that we go around trying to fix their issues without paying any attention to our own. Sound familiar? I'm definitely guilty of this, and I'm sure you are too! His warning to all of us in verse 2 is that the way we judge others is how he will judge us. If we're quick to accuse others, calling them out publicly to embarrass or shame them, and pridefully thinking we're better than them, we'll be in for a rough time on Judgement Day.

Interestingly, Jesus never says we're not to help our brothers and sisters get the specks out of their eyes. Helping each other recognize our sins is part of a healthy, intimate Christian friendship! He just says we have to focus on our own sins *first*. Then, when we do get around to encouraging others to recognize their sins, we'll come from a place of genuine humility and mercy. We'll be more aware that we're no better than they are. We'll speak to them respectfully as equals before God, not talking down to them as if they're worse than us. We won't condemn and judge them, we'll lovingly challenge and encourage them. We'll be more gentle and compassionate and patient with them.

Ask, seek, knock

Verse 7 is an incredibly beautiful and important promise. Jesus is encouraging us as God's children to talk to him about every need we have. We just have to ask. God is always with us, just waiting for us to bring our problems and requests to him. He loves to hear us asking, and he particularly loves answering us out of his overflowing goodness and power. And best of all, Jesus tells us here that *everyone* who asks God for help will receive it, with no exceptions. Just imagine a human father, proudly watching his young daughter struggling to tie up her shoelaces. That father gets so much pleasure from hearing his daughter's little voice asking for his help. By asking confidently, she's showing him that she knows he's there for her and will enjoy helping her any way he can. So ask your loving father for what you need with boldness!

Does this promise mean that God will give you whatever you ask for, every time? Not exactly. Remember, he isn't Santa. Read verses 9–11 again. Jesus promises that God *will* hear and respond to our prayers, and he says that God *will* give us good gifts. But Jesus doesn't say, "If you ask God for bread, he will give you bread." He says God *won't* give you a stone. This means he won't necessarily give us what we ask for, but he definitely won't give us something bad for us. Picture that earthly father again. If his beloved little girl asked him for McDonald's three meals a day every day, would he actually be loving her by giving her exactly what she asked for? The little girl is too young to understand the whole story. She doesn't actually know what she needs. But her dad knows about diabetes and heart disease and obesity, so he knows that what she wants isn't actually best for her in the long run. She might not enjoy the fresh vegetables and fruit that he gives her to eat, and may even feel like he's being mean by not giving her McDonald's! But that's because she doesn't understand that he's wisely and lovingly giving her what her body actually needs most to be healthy and strong.

Your heavenly Father is kind and good. He created the galaxies and the oceans. He exists outside time and sees all of human history from beginning to end in one glance. He knows you inside and out, better than you know yourself. He adores and enjoys you. He knows what'll be best for you today, tomorrow, and fifty years from now. So he might give you what you ask for, or he might give you something different. He might give it to you now, or he might tell you to wait patiently until the time is right. Jesus promises here that he always answers our prayers, it just might not be in the way we're expecting, or in the time frame that we think is necessary. That's why we have to trust that he knows best, as our loving Father.

Reflect and respond

1. *How does today's devotion change how you think about God?*
2. *How does today's devotion change how you think about your relationship with God?*
3. *Think about when you are most judgmental, and who you tend to judge most. How can you guard your heart against being judgmental this week?*

Everlasting God,
I believe that you are who you say you are.
I believe that you are the Lord of all creation, mighty and powerful and wise.
I believe that you are the God who hears the cries of his children.
I believe that you are the Father who loves to provide good things for his children.
Lord, help me believe.
Forgive me for thinking I know what is best for me.
Teach me to trust in your wisdom and plan and timing for my life.

In Jesus' name,
Amen

Meditation verse for the day:

Ask and it will be given to you;
seek and you will find;
knock and the door will be opened to you.
(Matthew 7:7)

Day 15

Opposite Paths

(Read Matthew 7:13–29)

In this passage, Jesus is contrasting a few opposite ways to relate to him. Think carefully and honestly as you read, praying God will show you which example best describes your relationship with him right now.

The wide and narrow gates

Jesus teaches that there are two ways to go through life: a wide, easy road to hell that most people take; and a narrow, hard road to heaven that not many people are on. So why is the path to heaven hard? As we read earlier, all Christians will face spiritual warfare and persecution for our faith. We're not only fighting against the attacks of Satan, we also have to fight against our own human nature. We all want to live life by our own rules. It's naturally easier for us to do life our own way. Becoming a disciple of Jesus means giving up our self-centeredness and recognizing that God is actually the main character in our story. It means fleeing from temptation, and putting to death our sinful desires. It means living and loving like Jesus. It means taking up our cross, which is to be willing to lose everything or endure suffering as we follow him. Not because we can earn our way into heaven by being a good Christian, but because we love God so much that we'll do whatever it takes to be close to him. Going against our sinful nature isn't easy, but it's the pathway that leads to life.

The true and false prophets

In verses 15–20 Jesus talks about people who teach the wrong thing about God and lead others astray. He warns us to beware of these people, as they often come disguised as legitimate Christian leaders, and it can be hard to identify them unless we're watching and listening carefully. In Mark 13:22 Jesus explains that some false teachers will even do miracles in his name. Just because someone does miracles doesn't mean you can believe everything they say about God! This is another reason why it's so important to read the whole Bible for yourself, over and over and over. The better you know God's Word, the better you'll be able to tell when people are interpreting it wrong, or even lying about what it means.

Jesus says in verse 20 that we can recognize these dangerous false prophets by their fruit. By fruit he doesn't mean apples or grapes, he means their actions and thoughts and words towards God and others. Their fruit is the way they live every minute of every day. That means we don't just listen to the words our Christian leaders say, but we also observe their character. Obviously no human being is ever perfect, but can you see the fruit of the Holy Spirit growing in them? Do they live lives characterized by love, joy, peace, patience, kindness, goodness, faithfulness, gentleness, and self-control? Do they practice what they preach? Do their lives glorify God, or glorify themselves? Are they humble and merciful? Are they peacemakers? Do they repent of their sin and hunger for God's righteousness?

The true and false disciples

Verses 21–23 are possibly some of the most terrifying verses in the entire Bible. Jesus warns us against thinking we're Christians when we're actually not. But the examples he gives of people who won't be allowed into heaven aren't stereotypical evil villains or violent criminals. They're people who say they know him well. They prophesied in church, casting demons out in Jesus' name, and performing miracles. They sure sound like Christians! These aren't even just the average Christians you might meet around your neighborhood; they're the people up the front of church speaking prophetically and praying over others. They're the people who seem to be amazingly spiritually gifted. They're the people who are Christian celebrities, who have best-selling books or popular TV shows. This is absolutely shocking stuff!

So how can we make sure we're actually real Christians? Verse 21 shows us it isn't about doing lots of amazing miracles, it's about doing the will of God. And what is the will of God? Jesus says it's simply to love God and to love others. That's how you know if you're a true disciple of Jesus. You love the Lord your God with all your heart, and you love your neighbor as yourself. Although he's using different language, this is actually the same thing as bearing good fruit. Think about that list of the fruit of the Spirit again: love, joy, peace, patience, kindness, goodness, faithfulness, gentleness, and self-control. Those are really just all different ways of loving God and others well.

But it's really important to recognize that it's not our fruit that saves us! Our good actions are not our savior. Our fruit is just evidence that we're actually trusting and treasuring Jesus as our Lord and Savior. Our fruit proves that our roots in Jesus are real. It's the external sign that something has changed deep inside us. As Jesus says in John 15:5, he is the vine and we are the branches. Branches can't grow any fruit unless they're connected to the vine. We can't bear real, lasting fruit without Jesus.

The wise and foolish builders

Jesus finishes his sermon on the mountainside with the story of the two builders, in verses 24–27. Notice that they both build houses, metaphorically meaning that they both hear Jesus' words. But the only house that lasts through the storm is the one built on the rock of a personal relationship with God. Simply knowing who Jesus is or what he says is not enough to save us. Jesus is warning us not to just walk away today, content to have read the Bible like it's just another thing on our daily to-do list. He's explaining that there's an eternity of difference between the person who just listens to his words and the person who actually puts them into practice.

Maybe you go to church, and highlight lots of important sentences in your Bible, or thoughtfully complete all the reflection questions in this devotional book. You might even lead a Bible study group or help out with the church worship team. But is that all you do? Remember, in God's upside down kingdom he doesn't look at outside appearances, he looks at what's on the inside. If you don't love and trust him, he isn't honored by how much you do for him. He isn't interested in how many 'good' Christian things you get done every day. He cares that he's first in your heart.

Reflect and respond

1. Are you on the wide path or the narrow path right now? How can you tell?
2. What part of Jesus' words about false and true disciples challenged you most, and why?
3. How can you make sure that you actually put God's Word into action this week, instead of being like the foolish builder?

Loving Father,
Thank you for making a way for me to have a personal relationship with you.
Thank you that your Word shows me the pathway to life with you.
I want to be on the narrow road.
I don't want to be led astray by false prophets.
I want to be your true disciple.
I want to be like the wise builder.
Please teach me how, for your glory.

In Jesus' name,
Amen.

Meditation verse for the day:

I am the vine; you are the branches.
If you remain in me and I in you,
you will bear much fruit;
apart from me you can do nothing.
(John 15:5)

Day 16

Jesus' Healing Ministry

(Read Matthew 8:1–17)

We've just finished The Sermon on the Mount, which was a sample of Jesus' preaching, and now Matthew is giving us some detailed examples of Jesus' healing ministry. The Bible doesn't include every single miracle that Jesus ever did, so as we read the next few chapters we have to ask why these particular stories were chosen to be recorded in writing. Most importantly, what do these examples show us about the character of God?

The man with leprosy

After preaching his sermon on the mountainside, the first person Jesus healed was a man with leprosy. Leprosy is a terrible skin condition, and back in Jesus' day there was no cure. People with leprosy were kicked out of their homes and forced to live on the outskirts of town, begging to survive. They were considered spiritually unclean and weren't allowed to participate in Jewish religious activities. Because people were so afraid of catching their disease, even their own family members wouldn't touch them.

This man has obviously heard that Jesus can heal his disease, removing the spiritual uncleanness that's keeping him apart from his whole community. Even though Jesus is surrounded by a large crowd, he manages to get to Jesus, where he kneels at Jesus' feet to ask for his help. His humility and faith are so obvious in his body language. Even the words he speaks are humble; he doesn't feel like Jesus owes him anything, or that it's his right to be healed. He effectively says, "I'm sick and want to be healed. I know you can heal me if you want to, but do your will." What an amazingly humble attitude!

Jesus' response would have completely horrified the crowds surrounding them. Jesus touches him. He actually touches the man with leprosy! Jesus heals people in lots of different ways in the Gospels, and he definitely didn't need to physically touch the man to heal his disease. So why did he deliberately choose to do it this time? This is a man who has been kicked out of his home, rejected by his friends and family, and looked at with disgust and fear by everyone who passes him in the streets. It's possible that nobody had touched him for many, many years.

But Jesus did.

Our compassionate God stoops down into the dirty, scary places where no one else wants to go, and he touches the untouchable. Our God abundantly answers our humble prayers with far more than we could have ever dreamed of asking. Our God shows us care and tenderness in our worst moments. Our God is a God of intimacy, of healing, and of restoration. He cares about the little details.

Jesus also touches this man to make an important point to the crowds watching. In the Jewish world of Jesus' day, people who touched an unclean person became unclean themselves. Spiritual uncleanness was contagious. Jesus is showing everyone that he's different. He's the only person whose *cleanness* is contagious. He's the only one who touches the unclean and the sick and the dead, and gives them his purity, and his health, and his life.

The centurion

In Jesus' day the Jewish people were part of the Roman Empire, and they were not happy about it. The Romans ruled over the them — sometimes very harshly — and there was regularly violence between the Romans and small groups of Jewish rebels who tried to overthrow their rule. A centurion was a high-ranking Roman military leader, but interestingly the parallel account of this story in Luke 7 mentions that this particular centurion had helped the local Jewish community a lot.

He is also the exact opposite of the man with leprosy. He's wealthy, influential and well-liked in the local community, with lots of servants and soldiers under his authority. And yet when he asks for Jesus' help in verse 8, we see that he approaches with an identical attitude of complete humility.

This powerful man knows all about ordering people around and making sure things get done right, and he recognizes that Jesus has much more authority and power than he ever will. He knows that he doesn't even deserve for Jesus to come into his house.

Jesus is absolutely amazed by this man's faith. Not by his money, or his power, or his military experience, or even how much he cared about his servant. Jesus sees this man's belief, and is honored by it. Our God doesn't value the things the world cares about, and he isn't distracted by external appearances. He looks on the inside. He's honored when we recognize him for who he really is. He's glorified when we humbly put our trust in him.

He healed all the sick

It's easy to read verse 16 about Jesus healing every single sick or possessed person who was brought to him, and wonder why God doesn't heal everyone who prays for a miracle these days. The quote from Isaiah in verse 17 gives us a clue why that might be. It reveals that Jesus did so many healing miracles in his time on earth, to prove that he is who he says he is: the Christ. His miracles demonstrate his power and authority over the created world, showing that he is God. They're evidence that he fulfils all the Old Testament prophecies about the Messiah. Jesus is pointing us toward a time in the future where all sicknesses will be healed forever.

This was literally the only time in human history when there would be so many miracles all at once. It was a very special and unique time, because God was making a clear point that Jesus is the most special and unique human ever. With that said though, you might be surprised to realize just how many miracles God is still doing around the world these days. There are millions of extraordinary stories out there, when ordinary people of faith like us get to see our God move in incredible, supernatural ways!

Reflect and respond

1. *How does Jesus touching the man with leprosy teach you about what God is like?*
2. *How has today's devotions helped you love God more?*

Most High God,
I don't deserve to come into your presence.
I don't deserve to be known and loved by you.
I'm in awe of the power and authority that Jesus showed through his miracles.
I'm overwhelmed by the grace and mercy that Jesus showed in his compassion.
I could never thank you enough for inviting me to be your child.
Lord, give me the faith of the man with leprosy and the centurion, so that I can ask for help with humility, but full of confidence that you hear me and love me and will respond with all authority on heaven and earth.

In Jesus' name,
Amen

Meditation verse for the day:

Let us then approach God's throne of grace with confidence,
so that we may receive mercy and find grace
to help us in our time of need.
(Hebrews 4:16)

Day 17

Being a Disciple

(READ MATTHEW 8:18–34)

IN VERSES 18–22, JESUS explains to some people what it will cost them to be his disciples. He tells one eager man that it'll mean leaving his home behind and moving around from place to place; not being welcome anywhere, never feeling like he truly belongs. He tells another man to leave his family behind while they're in the middle of grieving, before he's even been able to organize his dad's funeral. Is Jesus just being heartless here?

The cost of discipleship

Jesus cares deeply about this man's loss, but he's making a powerful point: following him will always cost us. Sometimes it will even cost us everything. Becoming a disciple of Jesus isn't a five-step program to being your best self, or a hobby we can just squeeze into our weekly schedule without changing anything else in our lives. Genuinely following Jesus will take all of us. All our heart and soul and mind and strength and passion. It will impact all our decisions. It will rearrange all our priorities. It will shape the way we think and the way we relate to other people. And as we've already learned, it will lead to persecution and suffering. If you saw this as an advertisement for Christianity would you still choose to become a disciple of Jesus?

Jesus is always honest with people about what discipleship will cost them, because he wants them to be prepared for the hard times when they come. If they're expecting the Christian life to be nothing but sunshine and rainbows, their faith will fall to pieces as soon as they face difficulties. Jesus also doesn't sugar-coat the cost of discipleship because he wants to test whether these people genuinely love him or are just following him because he's a good preacher who does amazing miracles and gives out free food every now and then.

There's so much more to the story of discipleship though. In this particular conversation Jesus is focusing on what discipleship will cost us, but as we read through the entire Bible, we can also make a list of the incredible gifts that come with being a disciple of Jesus. We get to be beloved by God! He frees us from our slavery to sin and shame and replaces our brokenness with his perfect righteousness. We're given an unshakeable identity as children and heirs of the King of kings. He fills us with the power of the Holy Spirit, offering healing and restoration to our souls and relationships. We're given a higher purpose and meaning in life: to enjoy God and share our enjoyment of him with others. In the middle of the storms of life, our peace and our joy aren't shaken because our treasure is safely stored in heaven.

The list goes on and on and on and on, literally into eternity. God promises us that there's nothing on this earth we could give up for him that won't be worth the sacrifice. Whatever the cost ends up being – even life itself – the joy of having a relationship with Jesus is worth it all! Do you believe that in your heart of hearts?

Jesus calms the storm

In verse 24, Jesus is asleep in a boat that's in the middle of a terrible storm. His disciples are fishermen who spend most of their lives on boats, so they would have been through hundreds of storms before. But this one is different. These experienced fishermen are freaking out, literally afraid that they're about to die.

We all go through times like this in life, where there's a storm raging around us and it feels like we won't make it through. We feel completely overwhelmed, like we're about to lose everything. It's so tempting to wonder if God is there with us in those moments, or if he even cares. We might feel like he's forgotten about us, or that he isn't strong enough to rescue us.

Jesus' disciples did the right thing: they called out for Jesus to save them. And yet when he wakes up, he says to them in verse 26, "You of little faith, why are you so afraid?" He can see into their hearts, and he knows that even though they've just witnessed him doing miraculous healings, they still don't really trust that he's able to save them. Even though they're begging him to rescue them, their hearts are filled with fear, not faith. He's saying that if they really knew who he was and what he was capable of, they wouldn't have any fear even in the middle of the fiercest storm. Their fear demonstrates how weak their faith is.

Maybe you pray a lot in the middle of your storm, begging God to save you. But do you truly believe he's capable of it? Do you trust him to do what's best for you? Do you know in your heart that he's Lord over the storm, or are you still filled with fear? Pray that God will give you the faith to have a peaceful heart even in the middle of a raging hurricane. Preach God's Word to yourself over and over, filling your mind with the truths that you know about who God is. Memorize Bible verses that help you fight against fear. Focus your heart on God, not on the storm swirling around you.

And be encouraged while you wait. Jesus was able to calm the storm with a single command. Look at the stunned amazement of the disciples in verse 27. They have never seen anything like what Jesus has just done! Your Heavenly Father is the Creator of the heavens and the earth. He has all power and authority over your storm. He is able to do more than you could ever imagine or hope.

Reflect and respond

1. *Being a real disciple of Jesus should impact every part of our lives. What changes have you seen in yourself since you started following Jesus? If you haven't seen any changes, take some time to pray about that with God.*
2. *How can you prepare yourself to trust God the next time a storm surrounds you?*

Dear Lord,
The Bible tells me that knowing you is more valuable than any earthly treasure.
Help me trust that.
The Bible tells me that your love is better than life.
Help me trust that.
The Bible tells me that you have authority over the storms in my life.

Help me trust that.
The Bible tells me that you are good, and wise, and trustworthy.
Help me trust that.

In Jesus' name,
Amen

Meditation verse for the day:

You of little faith, why are you so afraid?
(Matthew 8:26)

Day 18

God's Upside Down Values

(Read Matthew 9:1–17)

The man who is paralyzed

This story is absolutely fascinating, because Jesus' first response is not actually to heal the man who is paralyzed. The parallel account in Mark 2 says the man's friends had to break through the roof and lower him down into the room, because they couldn't push through the huge crowd at the door. And after all that hard work, what does Jesus say in verse 2? "Take heart, son; your sins are forgiven." Do you think the man and his friends were disappointed with that response? I definitely would have been!

Jesus sees beyond appearances to the heart of the problem. Anyone else looking at this man would see his disability and think that the thing he needs most in life is a healed body. But Jesus looks at this man and sees that his deepest need is actually spiritual healing. He needs forgiveness for his sins, and to be made right with God. His disability isn't his biggest problem, his sin is! Jesus does end up healing the man's body as well, to prove his power and authority to the people watching. But it's clear from this interaction that what matters most to Jesus is our relationship with him.

Have you ever begged God for his help and wondered why he doesn't give you what you want straight away, or maybe ever? Are you tempted in those moments to wonder if God really cares about you? Remember, the Bible promises us that God hears all our prayers and only ever responds with good gifts, because he's our loving Father. Maybe he doesn't help in the exact way you're hoping for because he's working on healing you in a different, deeper way first. Maybe he wants to give you something even better than what you're asking him for. Maybe he's using your pain to draw you closer to him, so he can heal your spiritual brokenness. Do you trust him to be giving you what you need most right now, instead of just giving you what you want?

Sinners and tax collectors

In verse 10 Jesus is having dinner at his newest disciple's house, Matthew the tax collector, the same man who wrote this Gospel. Tax collectors were Jewish men who worked for the Romans, collecting taxes on behalf of the Empire. Nobody likes paying taxes or being oppressed by a conquering army, so you can probably understand why tax collectors were seen as traitors. On top of that, they were often criminals too. They had a bad habit of taking more money than was actually due for taxes, and keeping the extra for themselves. Tax collectors were definitely not well-liked people in the community.

Look again at verse 10: "While Jesus was having dinner at Matthew's house, many tax collectors and sinners came and ate with him and his disciples." The people who are drawn to Jesus in this verse are people who live immoral lives. They have bad reputations. Their lifestyles and personal decisions are looked down on by the community. They get judged a lot. They get rejected a lot. But for some reason, lots of them really want to be around Jesus. They just can't stay away! Let's read between the lines here: they clearly feel safe in his presence. They feel valued by him, and welcomed at his table. He obviously doesn't make them feel guilty about their past, or shame them for their lifestyles. He's not taking every opportunity to remind them how sinful they are. He's simply enjoying their company and taking the time to show them how much he cares for them. What a wonderfully gracious and kind Savior he is.

Keep in mind that doesn't mean he's ignoring or approving of their sin. Jesus invites each of us to come to him just as we are. To bring our sin and shame and brokenness into his presence. He invites us to love him and be loved by him. But he never says, "Come as you are, and stay as you are, because you're perfect just the way you are." Instead, he invites each of us to be deeply changed as we spend more and more time with him. He welcomes us in no matter what, but sends us back out saying, "Go, and sin no more." He offers us a fresh start, and the opportunity to be transformed into something brand new, into the person he knows we should have been all along, the person he destined us to be before the beginning of time.

Jesus came to call the sick

When the Pharisees judge Jesus for hanging out with such sinful people, his response in verses 12–13 is really powerful: "It is not the healthy who need a doctor, but the sick . . . For I have not come to call the righteous, but sinners." Is he saying that there are actually people in the world who are good enough to not need a savior? Are some people righteous enough on their own? Of course not – none of us are – but there are lots of people who don't *think* they're sinners. They believe they're essentially good people who don't need anyone else to heal them. They're blind to their own helplessness or are too proud to ask God to rescue them. As we've seen over and over in Matthew so far, the people Jesus criticizes most harshly are the ones who think they've got it all together. The people who Jesus responds to with gentle mercy are the ones who approach him in humility, acknowledging that they desperately need his help.

I've often heard people criticize Christianity as being "a crutch." They think Christians are weak for believing we need someone else to give us strength and comfort and meaning. They argue that everything we need is already within us. They say we just need to believe in ourselves a little more and we can manifest our own healing. Jesus is telling us here that he really *is* our crutch. He's a crutch we can't survive without. We can't heal ourselves just by trying harder. We can't find what we're looking for just by searching deeper within ourselves.

Take a close look at the testimony of every faithful disciple of Jesus, and you'll see the same pattern: *we all walk with a limp*. We all know we desperately need a crutch. Read the sermons of the famous nineteenth-century 'Prince of Preachers', Charles Spurgeon, who publicly wrestled with overwhelming depression and chronic physical pain for decades. Read the powerful words of the bestselling author Ann Voskamp, who teaches us through her own pain how to grieve with hope. Listen to the honesty of grammy-winning rapper Lecrae, who humbly acknowledges his vulnerability and his fears and his struggles in almost every song. Read the diary of Mother Teresa, who struggled through periods of severe doubt and spiritual dryness. These are some really famous Christians, and yet they're the first to admit their weaknesses and their failures. To be a Christian is to admit you're sick, and you need a doctor. To be a Christian is to admit you're a sinner, and you need a Savior. To be a Christian is to know how helpless you are without him.

Reflect and respond

1. Jesus is called "friend of sinners." How can you be more loving and welcoming toward 'sinners'?
2. Meditate for a while on God's wisdom in giving you what he knows you need, instead of what you think you need. Do you trust him to really do that? Why or why not?

Heavenly Father,
When I think about your wisdom in knowing what I need most, I just want to worship you.
When I think about your grace and mercy in inviting me into your family, I just want to praise you.
Thank you for who you are! I love you!
Lord, help me to trust your wisdom and goodness when you don't answer my prayers the way I'm expecting. Sometimes I would just prefer to get what I think I need instead of the deeper spiritual transformation you're offering. Forgive me for not trusting you to know best.
Give me faith.

In Jesus' name,
Amen

Meditation verse for the day:

It is not the healthy who need a doctor, but the sick . . .
For I have not come to call the righteous, but sinners.
(Matthew 9:12–13)

Day 19

A Compassionate God

(Read Matthew 9:18–38)

In this passage, Jesus heals a bleeding woman, two blind men, and a demon-possessed man, and brings a dead girl back to life. Healing people was not the main reason why God's Son came to earth, and yet he does it over and over and over! He is travelling around the region, preaching to huge crowds of people to tell them the good news about the kingdom of God, but he is never too busy to heal someone who asks him in faith.

Jesus always makes time in his day for hurting people. He never tells them he's too busy, or that his preaching work is more important. He always takes the time to listen, and he always responds with mercy and grace. Nothing is ever too small for him. God is a personal God, who pays attention to the little details of our lives. He cares about our bodies and our souls, about our today and our eternity. He cares about our wholeness. Are there areas of your life where you need God's healing and restoration?

The bleeding woman

The woman who's healed by touching the back of Jesus' robe was too ashamed to ask him for help. She had a horribly embarrassing problem: bleeding from her vagina that hadn't stopped for twelve years. The parallel version of this story in Luke 8 tells us that she'd tried every other medical option and nothing had healed her. She'd probably spent every dollar she had. She must have been absolutely exhausted and had little hope left.

Under Jewish religious law she was considered spiritually unclean because of her condition, and wouldn't have even been allowed into the temple to worship God. She probably didn't feel like she was worthy of Jesus' attention, and didn't want the crowd's focus to be on her. Maybe she was hoping to quickly touch Jesus' robe and then anonymously disappear back into the crowd again.

Don't get the wrong idea here: Jesus' clothes were not somehow magic. Luke 8 tells us that the crowd around Jesus was so big he was being pushed from all sides, and lots of people were touching him all at once. Yet only this woman is healed, because she reaches out to touch him in faith, expecting his help. In verse 22 Jesus responds to her with love, tenderly calling her "daughter". He looks at her and sees her pain. He understands the twelve long years of suffering and hopelessness she's been through. Even though she can't find the courage to ask him directly for help, he gently replaces her brokenness with wholeness, and her shame with peace. No matter how big your hurt feels right now, let the kindness of Jesus wash over your hidden broken places. Hear him saying softly to you, "Take heart, child."

The harvest

Jesus is pretty much now a local celebrity, with crowds surrounding him wherever he goes. That must be exhausting and annoying whenever he wants to rest or just relax with his friends and family! Any yet verse 36 says that when he looks at the crowds of people following him he feels compassion for them. He knows that many of them are just interested in his miracles, and that some of these same people will be calling for him to be crucified soon. He knows that groups of them are judging him for who he hangs out with, spreading rumors that he works for the prince of demons, or that he's a greedy eater and a drunk. He even knows that some of them are already planning ways to kill him! And yet his heart goes out to them all in empathy and love. He sees that they're lost and he wants to be their shepherd, to guide them and protect them from harm.

In verse 37 Jesus uses the metaphor of a harvest in a conversation with his disciples. These are country people from small rural towns, and farming metaphors make a lot of sense to them. He says there's a huge field just waiting to be harvested, which represents the world waiting to hear the message of hope in Jesus. But he says there just aren't enough farmers going out into the field to do the work. Everyone around us today is seeking happiness and fulfilment. We know what they're really looking for is Jesus. But how will they learn about him unless there are Christians willing to tell them?

Interestingly, Jesus' doesn't immediately command the disciples to go out and tell the whole world about him – that'll come a bit later. Instead, he tells the disciples to pray for God to send out workers into his harvest. Verse 38 says that the harvest field belongs to God, and that *he* is the one who will send out workers. We have the privilege and responsibility to spread the gospel, but at the end of the day it's God's work. He'll get it done in his own ways for his own glory. He doesn't actually need us. He loves to involve us, but he isn't dependant on us.

Jesus is showing us here that prayer is the most important part of any work we do for God. It's where we need to start every day, every activity, every ministry. Prayer is our way of focusing ourselves back on God, and saying to him that we can't do anything without him. Prayer brings us to our knees, as we ask him to be our strength and wisdom. Prayer is where we communicate with God, relate to him on a personal level, and humble ourselves before him. This glorifies him more than any work we could ever do for him. Oswald Chambers, a nineteenth century pastor, once wrote, "Prayer does not equip us for greater works — prayer is the greater work."[1] We have to prioritize prayer before anything else. God wants and expects us to do good works in the world and spread the hope of Jesus, but he wants it to overflow out of an intimate, love relationship with him. He wants us to depend on him every step of the way, so that he can show us how good he is.

Reflect and respond

1. *Is there something you feel too ashamed or embarrassed to talk to God about? How does today's passage encourage you?*
2. *How has today's devotion challenged you to change how you pray?*

---

1. Chambers, "Greater Work."

Father God,
You created so many stars in the sky that we can't even count them all.
And at the same time, you care about the secrets in my heart.
You are magnificently holy and righteous, divinely majestic, perfect in beauty.
And yet you also humble yourself to listen to my deepest cries for help, and you love to heal my shame and hurt.
Thank you for all that you are Lord!
You are worthy to receive all glory and honor and praise!

In Jesus' name,
Amen

Meditation verse for the day:

The harvest is plentiful, but the workers are few.
Ask the Lord of the harvest, therefore,
to send out workers into his harvest field.
(Matthew 9:37–38)

Day 20

The First Missionaries

(READ MATTHEW 10:1–36)

IN YESTERDAY'S PASSAGE, JESUS told his disciples they should pray about God's plan for all the people still waiting to hear about him. Now Jesus sends them out into the harvest, not in their own strength or stocked up with their own resources, but with *his* authority and power. Eventually Jesus will send them out to people from every nation and tribe on earth, but in verse 6 he tells them to start by only going to the Israelites, God's original chosen people. His instructions to his disciples are filled with both strong warnings about what lies ahead, and beautiful promises about how God will help them through it.

Just like the first disciples, one of our responsibilities as Christians is to share the hope we have in Jesus with the world. Everyone around us is searching desperately for happiness and security and meaning. We have the ultimate answer to it all: Jesus! If we really care about the people around us, we should be excited to tell them how they can know Jesus too. Some Christians are called to become missionaries in other countries or communities, but most of us are called to be missionaries right where we are today: at home with our families; in our group of friends; or at school or work.

The warnings

Starting in verse 16 Jesus warns his disciples that many people won't be happy to hear their news, and will respond by persecuting them. This might include being thrown in prison, being rejected and betrayed by family members, and being hated by people. He warns that people will spread false rumors about them to destroy their reputations, just as they do to Jesus himself. He says that some of them might even be killed for trying to share the love of Jesus.

Christians in some countries around the world right now are being persecuted for following Jesus. Tens of thousands are killed every year, and lots more are forced to leave their homes or keep their faith hidden. For many of us, the risk of being killed for our faith is small, but maybe you're terrified of being laughed at by your friends, or being mocked by your family when you tell them that Jesus loves them. Maybe following and representing Jesus might put your job at risk. Don't let those fears hold you back from sharing the love of God with others, which is the most important, meaningful thing you can ever do with your life.

The promises

Jesus knew his disciples would be anxious about what might happen to them, so he also gave them lots of encouragement to strengthen their spirits. You might like to memorize these promises or mark them in your Bible so you can cling to them when you're being persecuted for sharing the gospel.

In verses 19 and 20 Jesus tells the disciples not to worry about finding the right words to say when they're arrested and have to defend themselves in court. He promises the Holy Spirit will be working in them to give them the perfect words at the right time. Now this doesn't mean that we should never prepare anything to say to others and just wing it – God gave us a brain for a reason! But we can take great comfort knowing that our loving Father has given us the Holy Spirit who's with us always, guiding us and helping us. Before we speak to others we should always commit our conversation to God in prayer, asking him to give us his wisdom to know what to say (and when to stay silent!) and how to say it.

In verse 22 Jesus promises his disciples that after they've completed the work he's sending them to do, they'll be rewarded. He's encouraging them (and us!) to persevere through the hard times until the job is done, knowing that at the end something beyond our wildest dreams is waiting for us. None of us know exactly what heaven will be like, but we do know that there will be no sadness or pain or tears or sickness, only pure joy as we enjoy eternity in God's presence. Jesus is not saying that if we work hard enough as his witnesses we'll earn our spot in heaven as a reward. He gives us eternal life as a free gift when we recognize our helplessness and cry out to him in faith. What he means here is that staying focused on heaven will help us persevere through the most difficult times in this life, because we'll know our suffering is only for a short time, relative to the eternal glory we'll have.

In verse 26 Jesus promises that one day God will bring justice. Anything wrong or evil that has been done against us will be punished appropriately by God. We don't need to be afraid, because God will defend us. We don't need to seek revenge because God sees it all, and he has our backs. Nothing goes unnoticed by our God.

Finally, I just want to encourage you to linger over Jesus' words in verses 29–31. Soak in them until they're in your bones. Jesus tells us here that our Heavenly Father loves us more than anything else in the whole of creation, and he's watching over us every minute of every day. In fact, nothing will happen to us that God doesn't allow to happen. The real stunner is in verse 30: "And even the very hairs of your head are all numbered." Jesus is saying here that the majestic Creator of the deepest oceans knows and cares about every single tiny detail of your existence. Not just useless things like how many hairs you have, but all the intimate things deep inside you that make you who you are. The hurts no one else knows about. The hopes and longings deep inside your heart. Your most private thoughts. Your loves. Your fears.

Many of us experience seasons of life where we feel very, very alone. We feel unknown and unloved. If that's you today, let Jesus' promise here be like warm sunshine breaking through the dark clouds. God sees you and he knows you. He knows the good, the bad, and the ugly. You don't need to hide any of who you are from him because he already knows it all, and in spite of the very worst things about you, you are still incredibly precious to him. He loves you so deeply and fully that he sent his beloved Son to die in your place. So don't be afraid of anything. You're worth more to him than you could ever dream.

Reflect and respond

1. How can you fix your eyes on heaven more this week?
2. What do verses 29–31 show you about who God is?

Oh Lord,
We live in a world of brokenness and pain.
Only you can fill the hole inside our hearts Father.
Being known and loved by you is what we were created for.
Forgive me for being fearful, and for not trusting you.
I want to go out into your harvest with your authority and power, not my own.
Give me your words to speak.
Give me faith in your sovereignty.
Give me the courage to sacrifice everything for you.
Here I am, send me!

In Jesus' name,
Amen

Meditation verse for the day:

And even the very hairs of your head are all numbered.
So don't be afraid; you are worth more than many sparrows.
(Matthew 10:30–31)

Day 21

Take up Your Cross

(Read Matthew 10:37–42)

Jesus' words to us today hit hard. They're radical words. Don't rush through them because they're uncomfortable. Expect them challenge you. Let the Holy Spirit use them to search your heart and show you areas where you aren't surrendering to God's kingship. Ask him to make today a turning point in your life as he brings these words alive to you like never before.

Jesus, our greatest treasure

In verse 37 Jesus lists off the people who are usually closest to us in the whole world, our families. Just imagine that Jesus names your most precious loved ones here. And then he says, "You have to love me more than you love them." That's *hard*.

Jesus isn't saying we shouldn't love people. The Bible makes it really clear that God gives us human relationships as a wonderful gift. God commands children to honor their parents and wants parents to delight in their children. He designed us to thrive by living together in healthy families and communities, and he longs for us to love each other generously. Jesus isn't saying this as a reflection of how little other people are worth, but to show us just how much *he* is worth. He deserves to be our most treasured love. He deserves to have our complete devotion and our full allegiance. Is Jesus number one in your heart and life?

Taking up your cross and follow him

If you think Jesus is asking a lot in verse 37, things only get more intense in verse 38. There, Jesus tells us we have to be willing to pick up our cross and follow him. There's no way to make this sound fun or pleasant. In ancient Roman times, crosses were a horrible way to execute criminals. Jesus' original audience would have immediately thought of pain and humiliation and suffering and death. Are you willing to face those things for the sake of Jesus? Are you willing to lose everything for him? To endure any kind of suffering for him? Or do you enjoy comfort and success and pleasure and popularity too much to give it all up? Is the good life on this earth too precious to you?

He's worthy of it all

Maybe you're wondering who Jesus thinks he is, to ask all this of his followers. Maybe you feel like he's being too demanding, or self-centered. How dare he say he deserves this much from us? If you feel this way, there's a very good chance your understanding of God is too small. Pastor A. W. Tozer famously wrote, "What comes into our minds when we think about God is the most important thing about us."[1] Tozer explains that seeing God for who he really is helps us respond to him rightly. Who we think God is changes our perspective on absolutely everything else. So, to help us understand why Jesus says he deserves to be the very center of our lives, let's take our eyes off ourselves for a while and fix our eyes on him instead.

The whole Bible is the story of God. It takes over a thousand pages, and hundreds of thousands of words to even scrape the surface of who he is! And even then, human words just can't start to do him justice. With that in mind, open up your Bible to Isaiah 40, and let's explore just a small handful of verses to see what precious diamonds they reveal to us about who this God of ours really is. As Isaiah 40:9 announces triumphantly, "Here is your God!":

- *He lovingly leads and protects us (verse 11)*: This beautiful verse says our God is an intimate, personal God. He leads and guides us with tenderness and kindness. He shows particular care for the weakest and most vulnerable members of his flock: the baby lambs and the tired mama-sheep who have just given birth. He gently lifts us up and

1. Tozer, *Knowledge of the Holy*, 1.

carries us close to his heart. Picture it for a moment. Doesn't it just flood your soul with relief and hope?

- *He reigns over all creation (verses 12 and 22):* These verses remind us that God created absolutely everything and rules over it. All the oceans on our planet are like a few drops in the palm of his hand. All the stars in the universe are like a tent he relaxes under. This poetic language isn't meant to be interpreted literally, but it's designed to help our brains get around the idea that God is more huge and powerful than anything we could even imagine. So next time you look up at the stars or gaze across the ocean, let a deep sense of wonder wash over you at the immeasurable greatness of your Father.

- *He knows everything there is to know (verses 13–14):* This concept is called God's omniscience. It means that he is all-knowing. He understands every detail of everything, ever. There is nothing new anyone could ever teach him, about anything. Not only that, but verse 14 tells us he knows "the right way" things should be. He is completely wise and utterly good, and his plans are perfectly right, every time.

- *He is the everlasting God (verse 28):* Everlasting is a hard time-frame for humans to imagine. This God of ours has always been, and he will always be. He is the Alpha and the Omega, the beginning and the end. He is where everything in existence starts and where it will all end.

So in just six short verses, we can already see so much of God's glorious splendor on display. *This is our God!* This is why the people in the Bible who see God's glory face-to-face instantly fall to the ground in reverence and terror, recognizing that they are wholly unworthy to even be in his presence. When we remember who God actually is, it makes perfect sense that he deserves to be first in our lives. It makes perfect sense that we should follow him wherever he leads us, no matter what it costs. No other response to a God like this would be logical. There is nothing in all creation that can compare to him. He's worthy of it all!

If you're anything like me though, you'll know how easy it is to lose this perspective of who God really is. We quickly forget about the holy reality of Almighty God on his heavenly throne, and get distracted by the bright lights and false promises of the world around us. A. W. Tozer's helpful advice is to "practice the art of long and loving meditation upon the majesty of God."[2] This means searching the Bible hard for glimpses of who God is, every single day. Asking the Holy Spirit to open your spiritual eyes up to see God's glory and beauty for yourself in the Word and in his creation. Praying the psalms and letting the words sink deep into your soul. Cultivating wonder at who God is, day in and day out. In addition to the Bible, there are lots of other excellent resources out there to help you fix your eyes on the awesomeness of God. Some of my favourites are J. I. Packer's classic *Knowing God* and Adam Ramsey's book *Truth on Fire*. There are also some great videos you can watch for free online, like Louie Giglio's "Indescribable" and "How Great is Our God", and Jackie Hill Perry's wonderful talk at the 2022 Passion Conference. Each of these resources will lead you back to what God tells us about himself in his Word, and will help you see him for who he really is.

And remember, the Christian life isn't about being miserable. Jesus isn't saying these things to punish us or take away our fun. He loves us and wants the very best for us! He promises in verse 39 that if we put God first, that's when we'll actually find life. We'll find a joy that is full and eternal. We'll find the person we were created to be all along. We'll find everything we've ever longed for. Because as pastor John Piper says, Jesus is "not a ticket to heaven; *he is heaven*."[3] Find him, and you'll find your heart's deepest desire.

Reflect and respond

1. *What stands out to you the most from today's devotions, and why?*
2. *What's the first thing that comes to your mind when you think about God?*

---

2. Tozer, *Knowledge of the Holy*, 116.
3. Piper, *Using Jesus*.

Take up Your Cross

Almighty God,
When I catch little glimpses of who you really are,
I see all of life from a different perspective.
Teach me to marvel at your beauty.
Teach me to bow humbly before your glory.
Teach me to delight in your holiness.
Teach me to wonder at your majesty.
Teach me to trust in your wisdom.
You're worthy of it all.

In Jesus' name,
Amen

Meditation verse for the day:

You are worthy, our Lord and God, to receive glory
and honor and power, for you created all things,
and by your will they were created and have their being.
(Revelation 4:11)

Day 22

An Angry Warning and a Tender Invitation

(Read Matthew Chapter 11)

John the Baptist spent his life prophesying that the Messiah was on his way, so can you imagine his excitement when he heard that Jesus was preaching with authority and doing miracles all over the countryside? His heart would have been bursting with hope that this was the Christ he'd been longing for! But he obviously had some doubts about whether or not Jesus was actually the Messiah, probably because he was expecting someone who would destroy the Romans in battle and lead the Jewish nation to a triumphant military victory. When John's disciples ask Jesus directly if he actually *is* the Savior, Jesus points to his life as proof. His miracles are the evidence of who he is. His teaching is the evidence of who he is. His care for the poorest and most needy people is the evidence of who he is. The way he lives reveals his identity. Can people tell you're a disciple of Jesus simply by looking at the way you live?

From verse 7 onwards, he starts getting angry at the people for not believing either John or himself. He says they've been given lots of chances to believe and repent, but even though John and Jesus took very different approaches in getting the same message across, both were rejected and ignored. John was a poor prophet wandering in the desert eating weird things and dressing in homemade clothes, and lots of people just dismissed him as being crazy or demon-possessed. Then Jesus came along, preaching in

An Angry Warning and a Tender Invitation

the synagogues like a normal rabbi and making friends around town, and people gossiped about him being an alcoholic party animal who hung out with inappropriate people.

The same is true today. Tragically, lots of people don't want to hear the message of Jesus, and refuse to believe no matter how the gospel is explained to them. They will always find a way of ignoring the painful truth about their own sinfulness. They will always find an excuse not to follow Jesus.

Woe to the unrepentant

In verses 20–24, Jesus says something very striking. He explains that the people who see him do miracles and hear his teaching but don't repent of their sins will have a worse time in hell than people from places like Tyre and Sidon and Sodom. Tyre and Sidon were bitter enemies of Israel in the Old Testament, and Sodom was destroyed by God in Genesis 19 after all the men of the town tried to sexually assault two angels. That's a *very* extreme example! Why would Jesus say these average Jewish people will be worse off than such evil people?

We know that all sin is evil because it's a rejection of God. But Jesus is saying here that some sins are actually worse than others, and as a result they'll be punished more in hell. We might expect him to say that the worst sins are things like murder, genocide, or sexual abuse. But he doesn't. Instead he says one of the worst sins is hearing and seeing the truth of Jesus and choosing to ignore him.

Read that last sentence again and let it sink in properly.

That's earth-shattering. Most of us have been taught to think of certain sins as better or worse than others, but from God's perspective it offends him the most when we know all about him and still choose to live as lord of our own life. That means hell won't be as bad for someone who never had the chance to hear much about Jesus, as for someone who went to church every Sunday of their lives but never actually truly repented in their heart. The more we know about God, the more we'll be held accountable for how we respond. Does that thought scare you? Take a good hard look at your heart and ask yourself if you've truly repented for your sin and are living with Jesus as your Lord and Savior. It really, really matters.

It's also worth noticing here that Jesus is very clear about the fact that hell *does* exist. In fact, he talks about hell more than virtually anyone else in the New Testament. These days, lots of people don't like to think about hell because it feels pretty harsh. Some Christians have even decided that hell can't be real, because it's much more comfortable to think about everyone going to heaven instead. We think that if God is love, he won't treat people like that. But justice really, really matters to God. In fact, it's a core part of who he is. Bible teacher Jackie Hill Perry explains it like this:

> "Imagine if we had a justice system that never executed justice. Where those who have murdered were not indicted. Where those who have stolen millions were not caught and kept from doing the same thing again. Where those who have abused the vulnerable, oppressed the poor, and failed to care for the marginalized were never confronted about their wrongdoing. At a fundamental level, we'd conclude that a justice system like that was unjust . . . but this does not and will never describe God. God's holy goodness means He must judge all wrongdoing. No matter how big or small."[1]

Because God is good, hell has to exist. Because God is just, hell has to exist. Because God is holy, hell has to exist. Because God is righteous, hell has to exist.

If you aren't sure what the Bible says about hell but want to learn more about this serious and important topic, I recommend reading the helpful book *Erasing Hell* by Francis Chan and Preston Sprinkle.

Come to me and rest

After listening to such a strong warning, the crowd around Jesus must be feeling pretty tense. Jesus is *furious*. He might even have been yelling! But Jesus doesn't just walk away at that point and leave them with his loud "woes!" ringing in their ears. Instead, he shows them what their alternative choice is. All of a sudden his tone completely changes, and in verse 28 he speaks one of the most comforting, tender invitations in the whole Bible: "Come to me, all you who are weary and burdened, and I will give you rest." What beautiful words to calm an anxious heart!

This invitation is the gospel in a nutshell. It *is* the good news. It's the most important invitation you'll ever receive in your life.

We bring our burdens to Jesus.

---

1. Hill Perry, *Jude*, 104–5.

An Angry Warning and a Tender Invitation

We bring him our guilt and our shame.
We bring our fear and our hopelessness.
We bring our sin and brokenness.

Jesus lifts it all from our exhausted shoulders and carries it for us, and he replaces it with the lightness of his righteousness, his rest, his peace, his freedom. This invitation is open to all, to come just as we are. We don't have to wait until we've fixed ourselves up a bit, or got our act together more. The only thing we have to do is recognize our brokenness and come to him in humble repentance, trusting he will do the rest.

Jesus is promising us here that the truest thing about his heart towards us, is that he's gentle and humble. Pastor Dane Ortlund has a wonderfully encouraging book called *Gentle and Lowly*, which focuses on the deep beauty of these verses. He explains that when Jesus calls himself gentle and lowly, it means he is "the most understanding person in the universe . . . Tender. Open. Welcoming. Accommodating. Understanding. Willing."[2]

In today's passage Jesus shows us our two eternal options. We can pridefully reject him and choose to be lords of our own lives, and face the terrible wrath of God. (God's wrath is his anger at sin.) Or we can humbly lay all our tiredness and our loneliness and our lostness at his feet, and be welcomed into the rest we long for in his gentle arms.

Reflect and respond

1. *Can people tell you're a follower of Jesus just by looking at the way you live your life? Why, or why not?*
2. *How does the reality of hell impact how you live and relate to other people?*

Lord God,
I believe you are who you say you are.
You are holy and righteous, magnificent in glory.
You are the God who saves undeserving sinners.
You are full of mercy, overflowing with grace.
I believe that Jesus is who he says he is.
He is the Messiah, my Savior, and my righteousness.

2. Ortlund, *Gentle and Lowly*, 19, 21.

He is the Way, the Truth, and the Life.
I believe that I am who you say I am.
I was completely lost and dead in my sins, powerless to save myself.
But through Jesus' saving blood I'm now alive and free from slavery to sin.
Now I'm your adopted child, cherished and loved.
Thank you!
Show me the parts of my life that I haven't surrendered to you yet.
Help me to hate my sin and to love obeying you instead.
Make me more like you through the power of your Holy Spirit.
I want to be all yours.

In Jesus' name,
Amen

Meditation verse for the day:

Come to me, all you who are weary and burdened,
and I will give you rest.
(Matthew 11:28)

Day 23

Jesus, the Christ

(Read Matthew 12:1–21)

Jesus is Lord of the Sabbath

Through all four Gospels we see a regular pattern of Jesus clashing with the Pharisees over the Sabbath. The Pharisees were strict and devout, and took a lot of pride in perfectly following all of the religious laws God had given their ancestors, the Israelites. In the Ten Commandments, the Sabbath was to be set apart as a holy day of rest, in honor of God's rest on the seventh day of creation. In Deuteronomy 5:12–15 the Israelites were commanded not to work on that day, and to take the time instead to worship God and reflect on his goodness to them in the past.

While the Pharisees were right to celebrate the Sabbath, Jesus was upset at their legalistic attitudes. Legalism is where people try to obey all of God's laws as a way of earning salvation, instead of trusting in God's free gift of grace. Legalistic people actually end up trusting in their own good works. They prioritize strictly following God's rules, but they forget God's good purpose behind the rules in the first place. The Pharisees were so obsessed with making sure no one did work at all on the Sabbath, that they made up hundreds of their own rules about what people could and couldn't do! They made the Sabbath a heavy burden to people. They focused so much on obedience to rules, they forgot the day was meant to be spent enjoying God.

In verse 7, Jesus says, "I desire mercy, not sacrifice." He's challenging them to focus on honoring God by loving the people around them better, rather than just carefully obeying the letter of the law with no mercy or compassion in their hearts. His response also reminds us that God gives us his laws for our own good– like taking time out from our busy lives to rest and be refreshed in God's presence! But so often we turn God's laws into a list of heavy spiritual requirements that weigh us down instead setting us free.

God's chosen servant

Jesus was aware he had made the Pharisees really angry, so he quietly left the area to give things a chance to cool down. He was aware they wanted to kill him, but he knew it wasn't time for his death yet. That's also why he tells the large crowds of people he heals not to tell anyone. He doesn't want his true identity to be discovered until the time is right for his death on the cross. He wants to keep a low profile. Matthew explains that this fulfills a prophecy in Isaiah 42, written seven hundred years before Jesus' birth. This prophecy tells us a couple of key things about who Jesus is:

- *His identity*: According to this prophecy, the Messiah's identity is firmly rooted in God's love for him. Verse 18 shows us that God chose him, loves him, and delights in him. Jesus isn't there for popularity or fame or the approval of people. He doesn't need his miracles to be the center of attention, because he's completely secure and content in God's love for him.

- *His character:* Verses 19–20 tell us that the Messiah relates to the people around him with gentleness and meekness. He isn't loud and argumentative, and he doesn't go around shoving his authority in people's faces even though he has every right to. Instead, he quietly and humbly works behind the scenes. The bruised reed and smouldering wick here are metaphors for people who are struggling or weak in their faith, and it says that Jesus is gentle with them. He doesn't put too much pressure on them. Imagine a person who's like a floppy, broken flower stem, or a tiny, sputtering candle flame which is about to go out. How incredible it is, that Jesus carefully and lovingly builds broken people up and tenderly encourages them to have hope, instead of condemning and rejecting them! Hallelujah!

- *His purpose:* The prophecy mentions the Messiah's purpose in both verse 18 and verse 20, so it must be important. That purpose is to bring justice to the world. Jesus is not distracted from his mission by the idea of becoming famous or gaining earthly power. He doesn't try to take the place of the local Jewish leaders, or wage war on the Roman Empire. Instead, he seeks to bring justice from the bottom of society up, by healing ordinary people, preaching the gospel to the poor, offering redemption to sinners and outcasts, serving others, and ultimately dying for the sins of the very same people who killed him.

Reflect and respond

1. *How does it change your perspective of God's laws to remember that he's given them to us in love, as the path to true freedom and contentment?*
2. *Is your identity firmly centered around God's unending love for you? If it is, how does it impact your life? If it's not, what is your identity built around instead? How does that impact your life?*

Father,
Thank you that Jesus is Immanuel, God with us.
He is the physical image of the you, the invisible God.
He is your character and your nature in a human form.
As I look at who he is, I learn about who you are.
Thank you for revealing yourself to me through him.
Open my heart to see more of who you are through Jesus today and every day.
I love you.

In Jesus' name,
Amen

Meditation verse for the day:

A bruised reed he will not break,
and a smouldering wick he will not snuff out,
till he has brought justice through to victory.
(Matthew 12:20)

Day 24

Watch Your Tongue

(Read Matthew 12:22–50)

The people surrounding Jesus are constantly gossiping about him. He's doing incredible miracles that are only making people's lives better, but the Pharisees keep trying to ruin his reputation because they feel like Jesus is threatening their authority. They whisper accusations between themselves, claiming that Jesus' miracles are actually powered by the prince of demons. Even though it might seem clear to us that the Pharisees are the bad guys in this situation, keep in mind that they were the spiritual leaders at the time. They are well-respected, deeply religious men who think they're doing the right thing by protecting their community from dangerous new ideas. They want to preserve their culture and customs from the revolutionary, radical influence of Jesus. They want things to stay the way they've always been. We're all like the Pharisees much more than we might like to admit, judging and gossiping about people who we think pose a threat to our way of life.

A tree is recognized by its fruit

In verses 33–37 Jesus says something very confronting which applies to every single one of us. He challenges the Pharisees to only judge a tree by its fruit. In verse 34 he specifically says, "For the mouth speaks what the heart is full of." He means that our words reveal what's hidden in our hearts. Jesus then warns us God will ultimately judge us all for the words that we have spoken.

Reflect honestly on the way you speak *to* others and *about* others. What do your words show about your heart? Would others describe you as an honest person, even when being honest is going to cost you? Or perhaps you're honest in a brutal, harsh way that tears others down, instead of striving to tell the truth in a life-giving way. Maybe you regularly make thoughtless jokes that hurt people. Do you only say kind words when you're in a good mood, and when things are all going your way? Would your closest friends be able to say that you consistently keep away from gossiping and spreading rumors, even if it's about someone you don't like or someone who has hurt you? Are you careful to choose words that are intended to build others up, or do your words have sharp edges on them that are designed to cut people down? Maybe the words you type online are bullying and cruel. Maybe you're careful to use positive-sounding words, but the tone you say them in reveals a judgmental or bitter heart. Or perhaps your constant grumbling and negativity show that your heart is not resting contentedly in God. Or maybe you just talk and talk and talk and talk because you pridefully feel like the world absolutely needs to hear what you think about everything!

Little kids say, "Sticks and stones may break my bones but words will never hurt me," but we all know it isn't true. Words have great power. A few hurtful words can sometimes change the direction of a person's whole life. The Bible actually has a lot to say about how we should use our words, because they have the potential to bring death or life. As broken human beings, none of us will ever be perfect as long as we live on this earth, so don't be discouraged if you still regularly say things that you know are not honoring to God of loving towards the people around you. But commit your words to God and pray that as he makes you more like Jesus on the inside, your way of speaking would begin to be transformed and renewed as well.

What kind of rats are in your basement?

The famous Christian author and philosopher C. S. Lewis once described his own struggles against his sinful tongue. He wrote that he would often speak rudely to people but then use the excuse to himself that he only spoke that way because he was surprised or angry or caught off guard. But then he was convicted that perhaps the words that fly out of our mouths when we don't have a chance to think carefully about them are actually the most honest evidence of what's really in our hearts!

Lewis used a brilliant example of rats in a basement to show what he meant. He explained that if you go down to your basement and bang around loudly for a while before you turn the lights on, you aren't likely to see any rats because they've all been given a chance to hide. But if you sneak quietly down to the basement and suddenly turn the lights on, any rats who live there will still be there, caught by surprise. The lights don't create the rats, and neither does the suddenness: the rats are there either way. The sudden lights just show the rats that are really there.

So think about those rats as your words. What kind of language do you use when someone or something suddenly makes you angry or startled? What about when you're really tired or stressed and your normal filter is switched off? The words that bubble up in those unexpected moments are the words that are already there in your heart, even though you might usually be pretty good at hiding them (including from yourself!)

Reflect and respond

1. What excuses do you tell yourself to justify speaking hurtfully to people or about them?
2. What specific sin has today's devotion convicted you that you need to repent of? Do you also need to ask someone other than God for forgiveness?

Merciful God,
I am so sorry for the ways I speak that dishonor you.
Holy Spirit, renew me from the inside out so that the words that overflow out of my heart are loving and gentle.
Make my character more like Jesus' character.
Make my words more like Jesus' words.
I want my words to be clear evidence that I am a child of God.

In Jesus' name,
Amen

Watch Your Tongue

Meditation verse for the day:

May these words of my mouth and this meditation of my heart
be pleasing in your sight, Lord,
my Rock and my Redeemer.
(Psalm 19:14)

Day 25

The Parable of the Sower

(READ MATTHEW 13:1–23)

JESUS REGULARLY TELLS PARABLES, short stories that often have multiple layers of meaning. The parable of the sower is one of Jesus' longest and most well-known parables. If you've already heard it a hundred times don't just skim read it thinking you know it all already. Pray for God to show you something new about himself and about yourself through studying this story again.

It's all about how you hear

The word "hear" is repeated fourteen times in just fifteen verses, which shows us how central it is to what Jesus is saying. He makes it even clearer that this whole parable is about hearing by finishing it in verse 9 with the instruction, "Whoever has ears, let them hear."

Jesus helpfully goes on to explain exactly what this parable means. He says the seed being planted symbolizes the Bible. The garden where the farmer plants the seeds represents all the people hearing God's Word. According to Jesus there are four different ways of hearing the Bible, showing that he's talking about spiritually listening with our hearts, not with our ears. These are the four ways of hearing:

1. *The path (verse 19):* Jesus says some people will hear the truth about God but won't believe it. They believe the lies of the devil instead. For

those people, it'll be like there were never even any seeds there in the first place. The message of the Bible has absolutely no effect on them.

2. *The rocks (verse 20)*: These people are excited to hear the gospel and they're keen to follow Jesus for a while, but they don't seek God with their whole hearts by investing time into reading their Bible or praying. They don't prioritize developing a deeper and closer relationship with God. They may go to church regularly, but the Bible's truths never take root in their heart. This means their roots are too shallow to survive the ups and downs of life. Even though their faith might look alive, when life gets hard their relationship with God shrivels up and dies, and they start looking in other places to find their identity and security and joy.

3. *The thorns (verse 22)*: Jesus explains that some people start out following Jesus but their lives are too full of earthly distractions. They don't give their relationship with God the attention it needs to grow properly into a mature, fruitful faith. Jesus says two of the main distractions these people struggle with are "the worries of this life and the deceitfulness of wealth." Notice that one set of distractions is negative and one is positive. On the negative side, they might be consumed with fear of the future, or stress and anxiety about any of the million things going on in life. The positive distractions are that they love life on this earth too much. They're too busy being entertained by everything the world has to offer to make Jesus the treasure of their hearts, and to build deep, steadfast roots of faith. These distractions mean their faith ends up being unfruitful.

4. *The soil (verse 23)*: These people listen humbly to the gospel and understand it, applying it in their lives. They seek God as their first priority and hunger for his presence daily. Jesus is their treasure and their delight. The Word of God takes root deep in their hearts and they dedicate time to strengthening their relationship with God day after day, year after year. Over time their faith grows to be like a huge crop a hundred times bigger than when it started. This beautiful idea of fruitfulness shows that a mature Christian faith is one that's shared with others so that it multiplies and never stops growing, transforming lives and communites.

Which ground are you?

In the parallel version of this parable in Luke 8, Jesus ends this parable by saying to his disciples, "Therefore, consider carefully how you listen." He's telling us that to apply this teaching to our lives, we all need to reflect on this question: how do I listen to the Bible? In other words, which type of ground am I? In reality, it's the most important question of your life, because it will impact everything about how you live right now on earth, and how you'll spend eternity.

Keep in mind that in the parable, all the people heard the gospel. Hearing about Jesus and knowing lots about him isn't enough. There are people who know the Bible back to front who don't trust Jesus to save them, so they aren't saved. Nowhere in the Bible does it say that going to church every Sunday makes you a Christian. The Bible says that just believing in God isn't enough — James 2:19 tells us that even the demons believe that God is real!

What matters is how our hearts hear and respond to the gospel. Do we have listening hearts? Do we respond to what we hear with humble repentance? Look again at Jesus' quote from Isaiah at the very end of verse 15: if we truly understand with our hearts we will turn and he will heal us. That is a glorious promise! All we're doing is turning. Turning means repenting and asking for forgiveness. Turning away from our sin and turning to Jesus. Turning means asking for help. Then he will do everything that's necessary to save us.

And there's more to the promise that's easy to miss. In verse 12 Jesus says, "Whoever has will be given more, and they will have an abundance. Whoever does not have, even what they have will be taken from them." He's promising that if we have a humble, repentant, listening heart, we'll be given more understanding, more wisdom, more growth, more fruitfulness, more of God. And not just a bit more, an abundance more! More than we could ever hope or dream! But his warning is that the opposite is also true. If we have hard hearts, unrepentant hearts, unhearing hearts, busy and distracted hearts, then we'll ultimately have everything taken away from us. We'll see less and less of God, and understand less and less about him. We'll end up with nothing.

The Parable of the Sower

Reflect and respond

1. Which type of ground are you, and why?
2. How can you and your Christian friends encourage each other to respond to the gospel with humble, listening hearts? What can you do together to develop mature, fruitful relationships with God?

Lord God,
Through your Word you're teaching me about who you are.
Give me a listening heart to hear you properly.
Give me a passion for reading the Bible and spending time with you in prayer.
I want to know you more.
I want to experience your presence more.
I want the gospel to take root in my heart and bear fruit in my life.
I want you to be the love of my life.

In Jesus' name,
Amen

Meditation verse for the day:

Jesus said, "If you hold to my teaching, you are really my disciples. Then you will know the truth, and the truth will set you free."
(John 8:31–32)

Day 26

The Kingdom of Heaven — Part 1

(Read Matthew 13:24–43)

In this passage, Jesus uses short parables to describe what the kingdom of heaven is like. In verse 11 of yesterday's reading, he explained to his disciples that the secrets and mysteries of the kingdom of heaven are not understood by everyone. This reminds us that the kingdom of heaven is not what people expect it to be. It's mysterious and surprising. It's hard to recognize.

The parable of the weeds

Thankfully, Jesus provides an explanation for the parable of the weeds in verses 36–43, so we know exactly what he meant by it. This story is an urgent reminder that the day of judgement is coming, and we all need to be prepared for it. This parable also tells us that the kingdom of heaven is actually already here, represented symbolically by the garden filled with wheat and weeds at the same time. God's rule and reign as King has already started, even while the earth is still filled with both good and evil. We might expect that when God's kingdom arrived all evil would have been completely destroyed, but it hasn't been — yet.

In fact, Jesus often talks about the kingdom of heaven as being both present *and* future. It's here right now *and* it's still coming. Both are true. It's happening in two stages: the first stage happened with the Messiah coming to earth. Jesus died for us, setting us free from slavery to sin, and he defeated eternal death once and for all by his resurrection. We're now living in the time between the two stages, when God is patiently giving as many people as possible a chance to repent and be saved. For Christians, the *power* of sin has been broken by Jesus on the cross, but we still experience the very real *presence* of sin in our hearts and lives. The devil can tempt us but he can't enslave us anymore! He's defeated but hasn't been thrown into hell yet, and he's desperately trying to drag as many people with him as possible, lashing out with his dying breaths.

Stage two of the kingdom of heaven is coming on Judgment Day, when the weeds and the wheat will be separated once and for all, and the weeds will be thrown into the fire for all eternity. There will be no more chances to repent after that. For those of us who are the wheat in the parable, there will also be no more sin, pain, or death, ever again. God's kingdom will be completely and fully here, in all its perfect holiness and glory, for all eternity.

The parables of the mustard seed and the yeast

In the next two parables Jesus uses two very small things to symbolize the kingdom of heaven: a mustard seed and yeast. He describes how a tiny seed can grow into a huge tree and a small pinch of yeast can make an entire loaf of bread rise, and explains that the kingdom of heaven is similar.

Most Jewish people at the time expected the Messiah to bring God's rule and reign to earth in a blaze of military glory, powerfully waging war on Rome and setting up a holy Jewish nation. That's the kind of Messiah that you couldn't really miss, even in the days before the internet. A triumphant kingdom like that would be obvious for all the world to see.

Instead, Jesus spent his time on earth in humility and meekness. He didn't start any wars, and he didn't forcefully announce himself as the rightful leader of the Jewish people. He was a servant King who washed the feet of his disciples, not a mighty warrior. He grew up in a tiny country village and worked as a simple carpenter for most of his life. He hung out with fishermen and prostitutes and tax collectors, teaching normal people about God, loving them as a friend and doing life with them. He raised a dead little girl back to life and healed a dying servant. He touched a man with leprosy and fed some hungry people.

Can you see why lots of the people around Jesus weren't convinced that he was the promised Christ? He definitely wasn't who they expected him to be. Jesus' revolution was unexpected, humble, gentle, and loving.

His kingdom is like a small mustard seed or a bit of yeast in dough; starting tiny but gradually working its way through the whole of society, bringing healing and restoration and reconciliation and love. Just think: that small group of disciples 2000 years ago has now become the worldwide Christian church of over 2 billion people, representing nearly every nation on earth!

Reflect and respond

1. Reflect on the fact that Jesus has already bought your freedom from sin and you now have the power of God living in you! How can you fight to remember this truth today?
2. What are some ways you think or act as if you're still a slave to sin?

Father God,
Thank you that you're trustworthy, and that your plan for salvation is wise. As hard as life is in this sinful world where there is so much pain and suffering and hatred, thank you for patiently holding off Judgment Day, because you want as many people as possible to have the chance to repent and be saved.
Thank you for setting me free from the power of sin.
Please help me live like it's true that I am dead to sin and alive in Christ. I'm a new creation in Jesus. Sin is not my master any longer.
I offer my whole self to you, to obey you and glorify you.

In Jesus' name,
Amen

Meditation verse for the day:

We know that our old self was crucified with him …
that we should no longer be slaves to sin.
(Romans 6:6)

Day 27

The Kingdom of Heaven — Part 2

(Read Matthew 13:44–58)

The parables of the hidden treasure and the pearl

Jesus' next two parables about the kingdom of heaven are the shortest but most beautiful in this entire chapter. This time he describes God's kingdom as a magnificent treasure worth everything we have. In the parables, these men both react by immediately and joyfully giving up everything else they own so the treasure can be theirs. Jesus is explaining how precious it is to have God as King over our lives, and trying to help us recognize that nothing else we have is worth anything close.

As we've heard all through our readings in Matthew's Gospel so far, Jesus is saying that becoming his disciple will cost us. The men in these parables don't just give up some things, they give up *everything*, and they do it enthusiastically. The beauty of these parables is that they encourage us that the cost will always be worth it. Always. What we gain when we follow Jesus will be far, far better than anything we've ever had to give up for him. In fact, we can even have overflowing joy when we give up our earthly loves for Jesus, safe in the knowledge that they're nothing compared with the peace and the satisfaction that comes with being a child of God (Philippians 3:8).

On top of that, Jesus is clear that what we gain isn't just eternal life in heaven after we die. In Mark 10:29-30 Jesus promises, "No one who has left home or brothers or sisters or mother or father or children or fields for me and the gospel will fail to receive a hundred times as much in this present age . . . and in the age to come eternal life." As God's children, we're promised heaven after we die *and* we get an abundance of blessings here in this life!

Keep in mind that these blessings are not necessarily private planes and a long, healthy life. Remember, God doesn't value the same things as our world, and his kingdom doesn't look anything like we might expect it to look. Jesus also tells us that to be his followers we have to die to ourselves every day, and carry our crosses. He says we should expect suffering and persecution. Those are not easy, fun experiences. Starting with Jesus himself, Christian history is full of people who were persecuted and died for their faith. Christians also suffer from cancer and miscarriages and depression just like anyone else.

But through it all we're offered a joy and a hope and a peace that overflows. We know the Living God, and are intimately known by him. We're loved unconditionally as children of God. We have a new song bursting out of our hearts that can't be taken away no matter what our circumstances are. We're invited to have our spirits restored and refreshed and transformed every day by the Spirit of God. We're welcomed into the presence of the all-powerful Author of Life to find comfort and rest hiding under his wings, like little baby chicks. What a privilege! What an honor! How can any earthly treasure compare?

The eternal weight of glory beyond all comparison

In these two parables, the men don't hesitate to give up everything they have for the treasure, because they understand its true worth. There are many millions of Christians throughout history who have enthusiastically and joyfully given up everything to follow Jesus wherever he led them, counting it as an honor rather than a sacrifice.

The Apostle Paul was a well-educated, powerful Pharisee and had many rights and privileges as a Roman citizen. Once he became a Christian, his life seemed to get significantly worse! He was regularly arrested and nearly killed by angry crowds; he was shipwrecked three times; he was beaten, stoned, and whipped; he was often hungry and thirsty and cold at night. The full list of his sufferings for the gospel of Jesus is in 2 Corinthians 11:24–28, and it sounds horrific. But somehow, Paul rejoices throughout his suffering, calling it "light" and temporary compared with the "eternal weight of glory beyond all comparison" that's waiting for him in heaven (2 Corinthians 4:17–18).

Jim Elliot was a missionary in Ecuador in the 1950s. He lived with his wife and baby daughter in a hut in the jungle with none of the comforts of modern life. He and four of his friends were killed when they tried to tell the local indigenous tribe about Jesus. He was just twenty-nine years old. In his journal a few years before his death, he'd written that he wasn't afraid to die for the sake of the gospel, famously saying, "He is no fool who gives what he cannot keep to gain that which he cannot lose."[1] He knew that life in this world is short, but that eternity with God is forever. He considered it to be a privilege to give up everything he had — including his life — for Jesus, confident that what he was gaining was more precious than any of it. I strongly recommend reading the book his wife Elisabeth Elliot wrote about their incredible story, which is called *Through Gates of Splendor*.

These are just a couple of examples, but history and our very own churches are filled with so many more. Read about Mother Teresa, a nun who joyfully loved and served the dying poor of India for almost her whole life. Be inspired by stories from the Underground Church in China, where millions of believers willingly face persecution with peace and joy. Be challenged by Corrie ten Boom, whose family boldly risked everything to save Jewish people and people with disabilities from the Nazis in World War Two. Discover the long history of African American Christians like Sojourner Truth, Harriet Tubman, Rev. Dr. Martin Luther King Jr., and John M. Perkins, who put their lives at risk to stand up against slavery and racial injustice in the name of Jesus.

Find out about the people in your own community who have risked everything to smuggle Bibles into countries where it's illegal. Talk to ordinary Christians in your church who practice radical generosity by fostering and adopting children from heart-breakingly tough backgrounds. Connect with refugees in your area who had to leave home because following Jesus could cost them their lives. Learn from people in your city who are so in love with Jesus that they move to poorer, more dangerous areas, just so they can be part of God's mustard-seed movement to restore and build up those communities. Hear from Christians who have deliberately chosen to remain single or childless because they feel God calling them to it, so they can serve him with all their energy and time. Listen to the stories of normal

---

1. Elliot, *Journals of Jim Elliot*, 174.

people who have given up high-paying, well-respected jobs to take invisible positions serving the unloved people on the edges of society.

Reflect and respond

1. *What is the most precious thing to you about your adoption into God's family?*
2. *What part of today's devotions challenged you the most, and why?*

Open your Bible to Psalm 145.
Slowly pray the whole psalm out to God, meditating on why knowing him is worth more than anything else on earth.

Meditation verse for the day:

I consider everything a loss
because of the surpassing worth of knowing Christ Jesus my Lord,
for whose sake I have lost all things.
I consider them garbage, that I may gain Christ.
(Philippians 3:8)

Day 28

A Day in the Life of Jesus — Part 1

(READ MATTHEW 14:1–21)

THIS CHAPTER GIVES US a detailed look at a very busy twenty-four hours for Jesus. His day starts with the bad news that John the Baptist has been killed by Herod. His reaction is to jump in a boat to try and get some alone time, but crowds of people follow him. Instead of getting frustrated, Jesus has compassion on them and puts their needs above his own. After a long, draining afternoon of healing people out in the wilderness, Jesus then miraculously feeds them all with just five loaves of bread and two fish.

The heading in our Bibles tells us that Jesus fed five thousand that day, but that's misleading. (Bible chapters, verse numbers, and headings were added into the text a long time after it was actually written, so don't pay too much attention to them.) Verse 21 actually tells us there were five thousand *men* who were there, but when you add in women and children the number of people crowding around Jesus that evening could have easily been at least three times as many. That's a lot of hungry people!

Jesus' miracles always point to deeper spiritual truths, and we should pray that as we read and think about them, God would open up our hearts to be able to understand that deeper meaning. Ask yourself, what do we learn about God from this miracle?

The Bread of Life

Throughout the Gospels, Jesus regularly uses bread as a symbol because most people can relate to it easily. His main point in feeding thousands of hungry people wasn't to show them that he could fill their bellies up with earthly food, but to remind them that he's able to fill up their souls so that they never feel spiritual hunger again. When we chase after meaning and joy from earthly things like relationships or achievements or possessions, we'll always eventually feel empty again. They'll always disappoint or fail us, and we'll need to find something else to feed our hunger. Jesus is the only one who can satisfy the deepest longings of our hearts. He is the only one we can find our wholeness in, and become our truest selves. He is the Bread of Life.

The leftovers

One of the most incredible parts of this story is not even the amazing patience and selflessness Jesus showed or how many people he miraculously fed, it's that that there were twelve whole baskets of leftovers! Was this an accident? Did Jesus get his miracle calculations wrong?

Jesus took the tiny amount of food the disciples could offer him, and he did a miraculous work of multiplying and providing. There is absolutely no way it should have been possible to feed that many people with just five loaves and two fish. But not only does verse 20 say that *all* the people got food to eat, it says that everyone ate until they were *completely* satisfied. No one missed out. They ate until they were absolutely full. No one had to hold back to make sure that there was enough for everyone else. And there were still plenty of leftovers! So what do these leftovers teach us about the character of God?

They show us that our God is a God of abundance. Abundance means you have plenty of something, much more than you will ever need. Our God takes the little we have to offer him — our broken hearts, our messy lives, our simple skills — and he uses us to do something beyond our wildest imaginations. Something better than we could ever dare to dream. No matter what we sacrifice to follow him, or give up in service to him, he'll give us more. When we spend our lives to love God and love others in his name, he will be more than enough for us. He will provide.

These leftovers also show us that our God is a generous God, even though he doesn't owe us a single thing. He doesn't just give us a bit of peace, he gives us peace that goes above and beyond any human understanding (Philippians 4:7). That's a level of peace that our human brains can't even begin make sense of! He doesn't just give us some joy, he fills us up "with an inexpressible and glorious joy" (1 Peter 1:8). The language of the Bible is so beautifully passionate and strong when it talks about how God treats us as his beloved children! His "comfort abounds" to us (2 Corinthians 1:5); he is "rich in mercy" towards us (Ephesians 2:4); he "lavishes" the riches of his grace on us (Ephesians 1:8). These simple bread and fish leftovers remind us that our God doesn't love us half-heartedly. He adores us, he sings over us, he tenderly woos us, he puts a banner of love over us. How could we want anything else?

Reflect and respond

1. *Reflect on Jesus' promise that he is the Bread of Life; that he will be all you need and will satisfy the deepest desires of your heart. In your life, what does it look and feel like to trust him to keep that promise?*
2. *What parts of God's character has today's devotions made you more grateful for?*

Loving Father,
Today I thank you for your patience and compassion.
I thank you that you promise to satisfy the desires of my heart.
I thank you that you promise to be more than enough for me.
I want to rest in your promises, and trust you with all my heart.
I want you to be everything to me.
Give me faith, Father.

In Jesus' name,
Amen

Meditation verse for the day:

Then Jesus declared, "I am the bread of life.
Whoever comes to me will never go hungry,
and whoever believes in me will never be thirsty."
(John 6:35)

Day 29

A Day in the Life of Jesus — Part 2

(READ MATTHEW 14:22–36)

YESTERDAY WE READ ABOUT how Jesus' day started: he received some shocking news, was followed by a huge crowd, compassionately healed people, and miraculously fed a generous dinner to thousands of people with just a few loaves of bread and some fish. But Jesus' day is not over yet, and he has a long night ahead!

Making time for prayer

When you've had a really hard, busy day, what's your favourite way to relax? Some of us exercise, some of us hang out with friends and family, many of us watch way too much TV. We might stress-eat a bunch of fried food, or collapse into bed early from exhaustion.

After his busy, emotionally draining day Jesus walks up a mountain to be alone with God and spends literally the entire night praying. That is absolutely incredible. Jesus loves God so much, that the best way he can imagine to de-stress and be refreshed is to pray for hours and hours and hours. He's had tens of thousands of noisy people around him all afternoon, and the first thing he does with his peace and quiet is to talk with his beloved heavenly Father. Pastor Francis Chan writes, "Prayer is the mark of a lover. Those who deeply love Jesus can't help but pray often."[1] Jesus' dedication

---

1. Chan, *Letters to the Church*, 114.

to prayer shows us that God truly has his heart. Prayer is where Jesus finds restoration and rest. Prayer is where he's filled back up again. Talking with God is such a priority for him that he'll even sacrifice sleep for it. This is a stunning reminder of the deep intimacy that exists between God the Father and God the Son; a loving family bond we're graciously invited to be part of! Isn't that the kind of relationship your heart longs for?

When we're exhausted, or upset, or just plodding through the daily grind, we can find our deepest rest by sharing our thoughts and feelings with God. We need to regularly step away from our busy lives and find a quiet place to talk with the Father who loves us. We need to stop filling our free time with so much mindless entertainment, and commit more of it to sitting in the presence of God. Then our hearts will be encouraged, and we'll be ready to face tomorrow.

Peter walks on water

These days we're so familiar with the idea of Jesus walking on water that it's lost a lot of its power, but don't forget to marvel at the authority Jesus shows over nature here! The disciples were right to be terrified. Jesus is supremely powerful, and that isn't something we should ever take lightly.

Peter is the boldest disciple and is often their ringleader, so it's not surprising that he's the one who ends up trying to walk on water out to Jesus in verse 29. And he was doing well at first too, keeping his eyes on Jesus. But what happened the moment he looked around him at the crashing waves? Fear overwhelmed him and he began sinking. When we're in the middle of storms in life, it's easy to get obsessed with watching the waves crashing around us. We focus on how strong the wind is, and how deep the water is, and how far we still have to go, and how unlikely it is that we're going to make it out alive. We feed our anxiety by fixating on all the things that could go wrong.

We should be focused on Jesus alone. If our eyes and hearts are fixed on who he is, and how much he loves us, and what he is capable of, we won't be afraid of the storm. We'll still feel it raging around us, but it won't have power over us because we know who actually holds ultimate power: Jesus. The beauty of this story is that Peter ends up being a complete failure, just like we all so often are. He gets scared and forgets to trust Jesus, and then he starts to sink under the waves. But verse 31 shows us Jesus' response, and it's so precious: "Immediately Jesus reached out his hand and caught him."

Jesus will always be right there beside you to catch you, too. He won't let you drown under the waves. Trust him.

Jesus calms the storm

Read verses 23–25 again, and pay close attention to the timing of events. In the evening after dinner Jesus sends the disciples away in the boat. Later that night the boat's already in trouble, being tossed around by huge waves. Just before the sun comes up Jesus heads out onto the lake, walking on water. So there are probably at least a few hours between when the strong wind starts out on the lake and when Jesus shows up to rescue his disciples.

When Jesus sent his disciples away in the boat, he already knew there was a pretty rough night ahead for them. Yet he sent them anyway. While Jesus was on the mountain praying, he knew his disciples were already struggling hard against the wind and the waves. But he waited a few more hours before he showed up to help. Jesus actually could have calmed the wind and the waves from way up on the mountain, or even stopped the storm before it began. But he chose not to.

The moment Jesus steps into the boat, the wind stops. It must have been an awe-inspiring sight, because verse 33 says, "Then those who were in the boat worshipped him, saying, 'Truly you are the Son of God.'" Jesus' majestic display of authority and power leaves no doubts in their minds about who he is. They know Jesus is God's Son. But if there had been no storm in the first place, the disciples wouldn't have seen Jesus work this miracle with their very own eyes. It would have just been another ordinary night. If he had calmed the wind earlier from his quiet prayer spot on the distant mountaintop, the disciples wouldn't have realized he was personally responsible for their rescue, and their faith in him wouldn't have been strengthened.

Have you ever been going through a hard time and wondered why God isn't helping you? Have you ever wondered if he cares you're struggling? Have you ever doubted his timing, wishing that he'd hurry up and rescue you already? Being a disciple of Jesus doesn't guarantee you won't go through hard times, but it does guarantee he'll be with you through it all. You might not sense him with you all the time, but you'll never leave his sight. You might feel like you're going to drown before he arrives, but his timing is always perfect, and he always has control over the wind and waves that are surrounding you. Maybe he's getting you into the perfect position to witness his glory and power in a special way. Maybe the struggle is necessary so your faith can grow stronger. Maybe by the end of the storm you'll be able to worship him with deep awe in a way that you wouldn't have before.

Reflect and respond

1. What does your prayer life show about your relationship with God?
2. Reflect on the authority and power Jesus demonstrates in this passage. How does it help you trust him more in your own hard times?

Lord of All the Earth,
You are the Creator of the waves and the wind.
I praise you that you are in control of every storm in my life!
Nothing is too big for you.
Next time I'm in the middle of a storm please help me to focus only on you.
Remind me who you are and help me trust in you, so I don't feel afraid.
I want to see your glory and authority demonstrated in my life.

In Jesus' name,
Amen

Meditation verse for the day:

When you pass through the waters, I will be with you;
and when you pass through the rivers,
they will not sweep over you . . .
For I am the Lord your God.
(Isaiah 43:2–3)

Day 30

Cultural Traditions vs. God's Word

(Read Matthew 15:1–6)

The Jewish religious leaders are shocked that a rabbi like Jesus isn't making his disciples follow their purity rituals. Jesus responds by accusing them of putting their man-made traditions above the law of God. It might seem odd that Jesus gets upset at the Pharisees for wanting him to wash his hands before he eats. After all, washing your hands is a good, healthy thing to do! But Jesus isn't speaking specifically against handwashing here, he's just using it as an example that points to a deeper issue. What he's really upset about is that these religious leaders are making up their own rules for righteousness and telling God's people they're just as important as God's laws. Not only that, Jesus says in verses 5–6 that the Pharisees are finding loopholes to get them out of having to obey things God *has* told them to do!

Our modern Christian churches have the same problem even today. There are things we believe and do simply because they've become part of our Christian cultural traditions over time, even though they aren't in the Bible. Do you know the difference between the two in your own life? This is one of the reasons why it's so important to read the Bible for yourself and develop a strong understanding of what it says. Don't just assume that everything you've been taught is biblical and true.

Cultural Traditions vs. God's Word

Traditions that honor God

Some of our man-made Christian traditions are harmless, like picturing the fruit of good and evil in the garden of Eden as an apple, or thinking there were three wise men, or picking December 25th as the date to celebrate Jesus' birthday. Others of our traditions are even valuable and good, such as saying wedding vows or having local church membership processes and ceremonies. These activities are also not mentioned in the Bible at all, but they still point to Jesus and can be done in wonderful ways that bring honor to God.

Traditions that dishonor God

But there are also many subtle ways our traditions can dishonor God, or make us lose sight of what the Bible actually says. For example, believing that Christians should have an allegiance to any particular political party is extremely dangerous. Our ultimate loyalty should only ever be to Christ, not to any specific political group. No political party or leader or ideology has ever fully represented the counter-cultural values of God's kingdom, and as Christians we need to boldly speak out against the unbiblical policies and practices of *every* political group. It's also good to remember that Jesus brought in a kingdom that was small and gentle and humble, changing the world from the bottom up instead of using political power to force his way on people from the top down. This doesn't mean Christians shouldn't participate in politics, but it's a reminder that all our hope shouldn't be in political movements to transform society. If this is a topic you're interested in thinking about more, I strongly recommend the AND Campaign's helpful and challenging book *Compassion & Conviction*.

Some Christians consider the King James Version (KJV) to be the only acceptable English translation of the Bible, refusing to allow any other version to be read. The KJV can be very hard to understand because it's written in old-fashioned English from hundreds of years ago, and many of us find it confusing. While there's nothing wrong with using this particular translation if you want to, it becomes a big problem when church leaders consider any one version of the Bible to be more important than making sure Christians can read and understand God's Word for themselves. Strict rules that keep people from knowing and loving God are never honoring to him.

Even the way our different churches organize themselves and run services can be dishonoring to God if we use it as an excuse to look down on people from different denominations in judgment and pride. Jesus says the world will know we're Christians because of our unity and love for each other

(John 13:35), not because of how we do baptism or communion, or what style of worship music we prefer.

The common habit of representing Jesus in art as a light-skinned man with flowing blond hair has also contributed to significant problems throughout history. Jesus was an ordinary Jewish man from the Middle East, so he almost definitely had darker skin and curly brown hair. Do you think so many people who identified as Christian would have owned African slaves, if they remembered that Jesus was not white? Do you think as many so-called Christian churches would have sided with the Nazis if they remembered their savior was a brown-skinned Jewish man? Do you think hateful prejudices against Muslims would be as common in 'Christian' countries if we remembered that Jesus looked more like a stereotypical terrorist than like the blue-eyed European hippie we see in religious paintings? And would our wealthy, safe Western nations be as unwelcoming toward middle eastern refugees if we remembered that Jesus personally spent time ministering in places like ancient Syria, which was right near where he grew up?

Reflect and respond

1. *Many of us regularly use religious clichés and catchphrases without stopping to check if they're actually written in the Bible, or even that they're based in biblical truth. Do you know which of these popular Christian phrases are actually written in the Bible? (Answers on pg. 120)*

		In the Bible	Not in the Bible
a	God helps those who help themselves.		
b	God works in mysterious ways.		
c	I can do everything through Christ who strengthens me.		
d	God will never give you more than you can handle.		
e	Cleanliness is next to godliness.		
f	When God closes a door, he opens a window.		
g	The fear of the Lord is the beginning of knowledge.		
h	Don't worry about tomorrow; tomorrow will worry about itself.		
i	Let go and let God.		
j	You are never more safe than when you are in God's will.		
k	Cast all your anxiety on him because he cares for you.		
l	Your breakthrough is coming.		

2. Reflect on how you went with that activity. Why do you think it's so important to build your life around solid biblical truths, instead of popular religious slogans?
3. What areas of how you live and think are more shaped by the culture you live in, than by the Bible? For example, think about what Christmas and Easter celebrations mean to you. Pray that God would bring other examples to your mind.
4. What personal goal can you set for reading the Bible more in the next year?

Our Father in heaven,
Hallowed be your name.
You are worthy of all praise!
Your kingdom come, your will be done, on earth as it is in heaven.
Please be Lord and King over my life, my family, my community, and my country.
Give me today my daily bread.
I trust you to give me everything that you know I need to get though today.
Forgive me for my debts, as I have forgiven my debtors.
I'm sorry for the ways that I prioritize human traditions over your commands.
I'm sorry for when I'm more influenced by my culture than by the gospel.
Please help me truly forgive the people who have hurt me, just like you forgive me.
Lead me not into temptation, but deliver me from the evil one.
Please protect and guide me, and help me fight off the attacks of the devil by the power of your Holy Spirit.
Help me to recognize the lies that my culture tries to sell me, so that I can resist them.

In Jesus' name,
Amen

Meditation verse for the day:

Why do you break the command of God
for the sake of your tradition?
(Matthew 15:3)

Answers: (a) Not in the Bible, (b) Not in the Bible, (c) In the Bible, (d) Not in the Bible, (e) Not in the Bible, (f) Not in the Bible, (g) In the Bible, (h) In the Bible, (i) Not in the Bible, (j) Not in the Bible, (k) In the Bible, (l) Not in the Bible.

Day 31

True Worship

(Read Matthew Chapter 15)

There's a lot going on in this chapter, but we're just going to focus on verses 8–9. Immediately after Jesus blasts the Pharisees for putting human traditions over God's Word, he quotes the prophet Isaiah at them, saying that even their best worship doesn't actually honor God. Let that sink in for a moment. These men know the Jewish scriptures by heart, and have dedicated their entire lives to being as perfectly obedient to God's laws as humanly possible. If they aren't actually worshipping God properly, have you ever considered that you might not be either?

Jesus says that the Pharisees do and say all the right things. To everyone else in the synagogue they look like the most holy guys there. They're leading and teaching others, they're confident praying in public, they probably know the words to every worship song off by heart, and everyone knows they always tithe exactly a tenth of what they earn.

But Jesus says in verse 8 the problem is with their hearts. Worship is not a thing we tick off a checklist, and it's not a routine. Worship is not just an action we perform in church on Sundays. Worship is a heartfelt response to God, an attitude that floods every single area of life. Worship is when we know and acknowledge God for who he really is, and reflect back to him some of the worth and beauty that he radiates.

Worshipping God in spirit and truth

In John 4:24, Jesus says that true worshippers worship God in spirit and in truth. To worship God in truth, we need to know him properly. We have to know the full truth about who he really is, instead of picking and choosing parts from the Bible to invent a god who suits our personal needs and preferences. We don't have any right to only accept parts of his nature that fit with who we think he should be. He is who he is. If we don't actually know him in truth, we will end up worshipping a figment of our own imagination!

Knowing lots *about* him is not even enough. The Pharisees knew plenty about God. It's like the way a person can know lots of information about a celebrity without actually having a real relationship with them. Being a Christian is about being in a personal relationship with the real God. It's about knowing him deeply and being known deeply by him.

Worshipping God in spirit means our hearts and souls have to be involved too. It's not enough to just think right thoughts about God, we should also enjoy him! We have to meditate on the truth of who he is until our heart sings and our mind is amazed, and we simply love being in his presence. We should find him breathtakingly beautiful. We should be in awe of his nature, and be desperate to experience more of his majesty. True worship involves our actions, minds, and hearts all at the same time.

Be careful though: it's easy to get caught up in the emotional whirlwind of a powerful worship song, or a passionate altar call. Make sure that your emotions when you worship aren't just the soaring, heart-bursting feelings you might also get at a concert by your favourite band or after an inspiring motivational speech. In true worship, our emotions aren't centered on how good we feel, but are totally focused on how great God is, celebrating who he truly is and has been and will be for all eternity.

But what is worship?

It's common to think that worship means singing Christian songs. Music is definitely found all through Bible as an important way we can worship God, but it's not the only way.

In Romans 12:1, Paul encourages Christians to "offer your bodies as a living sacrifice, holy and pleasing to God – this is your true and proper worship." So Paul is saying that anything we do can be a way of worshipping God, as long as it's done in spirit and truth, out of reverent love for God! This means you can worship God by playing sport, creating art, or caring for a sick baby. You can worship him by admiring the beauty of nature, baking something delicious, studying hard, or even by simply doing the washing up. There's a fantastic description in 2 Samuel 6:14 of King David worshipping by "dancing before the Lord with all his might" down the middle of the street!

There are some very special and important things about meeting together with other Christians and worshipping God together at church by singing and tithing and praying. We can't do the Christian life without it! But worship doesn't only happen on Sunday mornings. When our bodies, minds, and hearts are focused on treasuring God above anything else, all of life can be worship.

Reflect and respond

1. *How does today's devotions change how you think about worshipping God?*
2. *Think about your plans for the next few days. How can you offer yourself as a living sacrifice to God, worshipping him through all the activities that you have planned?*

Almighty God,
I love you, and I want my life to be a living sacrifice to you.
I want to worship you in truth, understanding who you have revealed yourself to be in your Word.
I want to worship you in spirit, with all my heart and soul.
Show me how to make my whole life a love song to you.

In Jesus' name,
Amen

Meditation verse for the day:

Offer your bodies as a living sacrifice,
holy and pleasing to God –
this is your true and proper worship.
(Romans 12:1)

Day 32

Understanding Spiritual Truths

(Read Matthew Chapter 16)

This is a really encouraging chapter for any of us who find the Bible hard to understand. It reminds us that even Jesus' closest followers often missed the point completely, but that he still included them in his beautiful plan to save the world.

By this stage Jesus has been traveling around the countryside for quite a while. He's done so many incredible miracles and his handpicked group of disciples have been right there next to him the entire time, watching and hearing everything. You'd think they would understand him better than anyone by now! But in verse 7 they still completely misinterpret his warning about the religious leaders, thinking that he's telling them off for forgetting to bring bread. No wonder Jesus is frustrated with them. He can't believe they've literally just watched him miraculously feed thousands of people with a few loaves and fish and still think he's worried about where lunch is coming from!

Why does Jesus speak in parables?

As we've seen throughout the book of Matthew, Jesus regularly talks in parables. This is definitely not the only time Jesus' metaphorical sayings are misunderstood by people who think he's speaking literally. So if Jesus wants people to understand what he has to say, why doesn't he just say it simply and clearly? The disciples actually asked Jesus that same question back in

Matthew 13:10, and he answered that only people who have humble, listening hearts will understand the things he talks about. It's all about how we hear. Every time we approach God's Word we have to take care that our hearts are repentant and humble. Many people hear the truth of God's kingdom but not everyone is paying attention, just like Jesus showed in the parable of the sower back in chapter 13. Some people won't believe it. Some people will be distracted away. Some will give up when it gets too hard. Some will choose to go their own way.

The Holy Spirit teaches us

Maybe you're listening closely to Jesus and desperately want to understand what the Bible says, but it just seems too complicated and difficult. After all, lots of very clever people have dedicated their entire lives to studying what the Bible means. People write books arguing over the meaning of a single verse! It's not the easiest book to read. But don't give up trying, because verse 17 gives us a great encouragement.

Simon Peter (also known as Peter) has already failed Jesus a few times and will fail him again in a devastating way right before Jesus' death. Only a few verses after this, in verse 22, Jesus has to harshly criticize Peter for being way out of line! And yet in verse 16, Peter shows that he understands Jesus is truly the Messiah. Jesus says that Peter only knows this deep spiritual truth because God himself revealed it to him. Not only that, but in verse 18 Jesus then promises that Peter will be the person who starts building up the Christian church all around the world! What an honor for an uneducated fisherman who sometimes can't seem to get some pretty basic spiritual things right. In spite of all his weaknesses and failures, Peter ended up writing two of the books of the New Testament and has been known throughout history as one of the first leaders of the early Christian church.

So even if you struggle to understand the Bible, you can still have life's greatest treasure: to know God and be known by him. In Matthew 11:25 Jesus says that in his upside-down kingdom, God hides the truth from the world's smartest people and reveals it to little children. God avoids the proud who think they've got it all together, and gives himself to the humble who know they desperately need him. Our world values intelligence, and rewards people who are very clever and talented. But God deliberately chooses to do things the opposite way. All through the Bible and in history he's used the least likely people to do the most amazing things for his glory.

So how exactly will God help you understand the Bible and get to know him better? Jesus promises that every single Christian has received his Holy Spirit to live in us and teach us the truth about God through the Bible. Jesus actually even says in John 16:7 that it's better for us to have the Holy Spirit teaching us than to have Jesus himself on earth with us! How incredible is that? If God's Spirit can help an uneducated guy like Peter understand who Jesus is, he can do the same with you. If the Holy Spirit could turn Peter into one of the most important people in church history, he can also do amazing things with your life, as long as you have a humble, listening heart.

So before you read the Bible every day, pray for the Holy Spirit to open up your mind to be able to see and understand what God wants you to know. Practice sitting quietly, meditating on Scripture and listening to what the Holy Spirit is teaching you. Find a strong Christian mentor who can help you understand some of the trickier parts the Bible. And never give up seeking to know God more intimately: he's worth it.

Reflect and respond

1. What do you personally find hardest to understand about the Bible and/or God?
2. What steps will you take this week to find biblical, trustworthy, wise answers to the questions you have?
3. Reflect on Jesus' promise that having his Holy Spirit is better than having him physically by your side. Do you believe him? How does/would it impact your life if you really trust in that promise?

Understanding Spiritual Truths

Heavenly Father,
In the Bible, you promise that if I seek you with all my heart, I will find you.
Please help me seek you with all my heart because I want to find you.
You promise to give me the Holy Spirit, to teach me who you are.
Please help me experience the presence of the Holy Spirit in a very real way today.
Open up my eyes and my ears to understand the Bible,
so that I can know you better.
Your Word says that you use foolish and weak people to bring honor to your name.
Please keep your promises to me.

In Jesus' name,
Amen

Meditation verse for the day:

When he, the Spirit of truth, comes,
he will guide you into all the truth.
(John 16:13)

Day 33

The Transfiguration

(READ MATTHEW 17:1–13)

IN THIS PASSAGE SOMETHING absolutely incredible happens: Jesus goes up onto a mountainside with his inner circle of disciples and is transfigured. To be transfigured means his appearance is transformed into something beautiful. His face becomes as bright as the sun and his clothes are like a shining white light! The disciples would have literally struggled to even look at him. Not only that, he's suddenly talking with two of the great figures in Jewish history — Moses and Elijah — who have both been dead for hundreds of years! And as if that weren't enough, God himself speaks to them out of the cloud. No wonder the disciples were absolutely overwhelmed with terror and awe.

Who is Jesus?

We know from the previous chapter of Matthew that many people at that time weren't entirely sure who Jesus was. It even took his disciples a long time to understand that he was the Messiah they'd been waiting for, because he was so different from what they were expecting. In this passage, God gives the disciples a little glimpse of who Jesus really is. He's the eternal Son of the Living God, who has existed in glory with God from before the beginning of time. He's the Word through whom God made all of creation. On this mountain the disciples suddenly get to see a tiny reflection of Jesus' true majesty. Jesus' transfiguration is a little preview of what heaven will be

The Transfiguration

like, when we won't need the sun anymore because the radiant glory of God and Jesus will be our light instead (Revelation 21:23).

The Trinity

There's also something else we need to understand here about who Jesus is. Jesus is God's beloved Son, but Jesus is also God. He's both at the same time. Colossians 2:9 tells us that Jesus is the fullness of God — everything about who God is — in a human being. Colossians 1:15 says that Jesus is the "image of the invisible God." This means that God is an invisible spirit and doesn't have a body, but when we look at Jesus we are seeing the physical picture of who God is spiritually. When we learn about the character of Jesus from his actions and his words, we're learning about who God is too. It's why the light shining from Jesus' face on the top of the mountain is literally "the radiance of God's glory" (Hebrews 1:3). Jesus' glory *is* God's glory. Jesus is Immanuel: God with us. That's why Jesus says, "Anyone who has seen me has seen the Father . . . I am in the Father and the Father is in me" (John 14:9,11). God gave us Jesus to reveal himself to us in a way we can understand, through a human body with human words and human actions.

This concept is part of what is called the Trinity. Trinity is not a word you'll find written anywhere in the Bible, but it is a word used by Christians to explain the mysterious way the whole Bible shows God is three persons in one: God the Father, God the Son, and God the Holy Spirit. They aren't one God with three different roles, or three Gods who all work together. They are all fully God and they are all equal and eternal, but they are also all unique beings.

In his wonderful book *Knowing God*, J. I. Packer explores the Trinity in lots of helpful detail. He uses Scripture to show that the nature of God the Father is to plan and direct all things according to his will, the nature of God the Son is to "find all his joy in doing his Father's will"[1], and the nature of God the Spirit is to act in the world as a witness to both the Father and the Son. Packer describes Jesus and the Holy Spirit as being the power of God in action.

If you feel like your head's hurting from trying to understand how the Trinity works, you aren't alone. The Trinity isn't humanly possible, but God is not human. He is more than our brains can properly comprehend, and much bigger than words could ever explain. But thankfully we don't need

---

1. Packer, *Knowing God*, 69.

to fully understand God. Just let the complexity and hugeness of the Trinity lead you to marvel at our God, and worship him in reverence and awe. He is beyond all understanding!

The love dance

The most beautiful thing about the Trinity is something the disciples are given a glimpse of on the mountaintop: the incredible love that exists between God the Father, God the Son, and God the Holy Spirit. In verse 5 the Father's voice came out of the cloud and said, "This is my Son, whom I love; with him I am well pleased." These are simple words, but they hint at the very deep, important truth that God the Father adores his Son. He delights in Jesus, and takes pleasure in him. Jesus honors his Father and the Father honors Jesus. The Holy Spirit glorifies them both. This is why Jesus spends so many hours praying – he just loves spending quality time with his Father!

C. S. Lewis described this loving relationship as a beautiful dance, where the Father, Son, and Holy Spirit each spend eternity adoring, exalting, and selflessly serving one another. They are complete and whole and gloriously joyful. They don't need anything from anyone else, and have been that way for all of existence. Lewis explains that this dance is the most important thing in the world for us, because loving and being loved are at the very center of God's nature. God is love, and we're made in the image of God. This means that loving and being loved are also at the very core of who we are as human beings. Love is our reason for existing!

This is why we all seek fulfilment and satisfaction through relationships. We were created to be made whole through deep, intimate, relational love. We're designed to find our truest meaning in loving and being loved. And God is perfect love, so it's only inside a relationship with him that our souls will find true, lasting joy.

Reflect and respond

1. *We like to think of Jesus as our loving best friend, which he is! But we're reminded in this passage that Jesus is also God: blindingly magnificent in eternal holiness and majesty and power. How does thinking about Jesus in this way change how you approach him in your heart?*

The Transfiguration

2. *Reflect on the fact that perfect love is at the center of who God is. How does this encourage you today?*

Loving God,
I want to know you more.
My deepest desire is to experience more of your presence.
Teach me who you are.
Show me your glory.
Captivate me with your beauty and splendor.
Amaze me with your power and wisdom.
Humble me with your holiness and righteousness.
Satisfy me with your goodness and faithfulness.
Overwhelm me with your perfect love.
I'm desperate to see your face.
Please give me eyes to see you, and ears to hear you.

In Jesus' name,
Amen

Meditation verse for the day:

The Son is the radiance of God's glory
and the exact representation of his being,
sustaining all things by his powerful word.
(Hebrews 1:3)

Day 34

A Mustard Seed of Faith

(READ MATTHEW 17:14–27)

AFTER THE AMAZING AND terrifying experience witnessing Jesus' divine glory on the mountaintop, the three disciples must have been pumped full of adrenaline and giddy with excitement. They had literally just heard God the Father's voice speaking! They had seen Moses and Elijah! That's a once-in-a-lifetime experience. Then they headed back into town with Jesus, only to find out the other disciples hadn't been able to drive a demon out of a little boy. This is the heart-breaking reality of life here on earth.

We can move mountains

In verse 20, Jesus tells his disciples that all they needed was a tiny bit of faith to heal the boy. By saying this, he's telling the disciples their problem isn't actually the amount of faith they have. He symbolically contrasts two opposite things, tiny mustard seeds and huge mountains, to show them that what actually matters is *who our faith is in*. Even small, weak faith is enough to do the biggest miracles imaginable, because it's not our faith that has any power; it's God.

Imagine you're climbing a tree and the branch above you is a rotten little twig. Does it make a difference if you believe with your whole heart that the twig will be able to support your weight? Nope. No matter how strong your faith is in that little branch, it'll still break when you try to hold onto it because it's just too weak to hold you up. Your faith is in the wrong thing, so it counts for nothing and you're going to fall. Jesus says it's not about how powerful our faith is; the only thing that matters is that our faith is in him alone. That's because it's not our strong faith that will do miracles, but God's amazing power and mercy working through us. He's the one who moves mountains, not us.

Not every mountain will move

Jesus clearly says here that nothing is impossible for those who have faith in God. It's very easy to take Jesus' words here to mean that we'll be able to perform every single miracle that we ever try in Jesus' name, as long as we believe in him. But is that actually the whole story? Like with any topic, it's really important we read this one sentence in the context of the entire Bible. Think of the Bible like thousands of tiny puzzle pieces; we can't just look at one small piece and understand the whole picture. The Bible tells us over and over and over hundreds of times that God is sovereign over everything, so we know that's definitely part of the puzzle's big picture. Nothing is impossible for him. But does God heal everyone in the whole Bible? Does God take away every bit of suffering from his people as soon as they ask? Does God answer every faith-filled prayer with a "Yes!" right then and there? Does every single faithful Christian live a long, healthy life and die happily in their sleep at a ripe old age? There are hundreds of examples we could examine, but let's just look at the life of Jesus himself to find out.

Right before he was arrested to be killed, Jesus prayed in the garden of Gethsemane. Matthew 26 tells us that he was so overwhelmed with sadness he felt like he would die, and he begged God to stop his crucifixion. He knew what was about to happen to him and he was desperate for another way.

Did Jesus have at least a mustard seed of faith in God? He sure did! Did God love Jesus? Absolutely! But did God perform a miracle and answer Jesus' prayer that night by rescuing him from death? He definitely did not. We can see here that just because God *can* perform any miracle doesn't mean he necessarily *will* do it.

In Matthew 7 Jesus taught us that our loving Father will only give us things that are good for us. At the time of Jesus' death, it seemed like a terrible, unjust thing to happen, and yet we know that through it the whole world was offered salvation. Jesus' death was actually the single greatest event in human history! That's why we commemorate the day of his death as *Good* Friday. It was a wonderful day for all of humanity.

It's also important to notice how Jesus prayed in Gethsemane that awful night: twice he said to God, "Your will be done." God does not do miracles for or through us unless it's his will. We might think the mountain needs to move, but only he knows best. If he leaves that mountain right where it is, we have to trust that it's for a good reason. Only he sees the whole story and knows what will make us most like Jesus and bring him the most glory in the long run. It can be extremely hard for us to ever understand why God lets people we love die, or lets us go through traumatic experiences, or lets horrible catastrophes happen around the world. But that's because we're not God. We will never be able to understand everything that he can understand. If he doesn't do the miracle that you're faithfully praying for, do you trust that he has a better plan?

Pray big

There are lots of reasons in the Bible why God might choose not to move a mountain for us, even if we faithfully pray for it. However, in his great mercy God regularly blesses us and answers our prayers even though we don't deserve it. We see that over and over again in the Bible and in our own lives. So do you really believe Jesus' words in verse 20? Do you expect to see God do miracles? Is your very first reaction when you face a problem to fall to your knees in faith and humility and complete dependence on God? Do you believe that he can do impossible things in your life and your community? Do you pray with the confident hope that you'll see God's power displayed in an amazing way?

Sometimes we fall into the trap of praying half-heartedly without really expecting God to answer. Maybe we just pray out of habit, or we keep our prayers small so we won't be disappointed. Maybe we imagine God is a human like us, with limitations and boundaries on his power, so we don't expect too much from him. But James 5:16 promises us that "the prayer of a righteous person is powerful and effective."

So pray humbly, but pray boldly. Pray asking for God's glory to be displayed when he does the impossible in your life. Pray for a testimony of his faithfulness and goodness. Pour your heart's desires out to God and then pray for his will to be done, like Jesus did. Pray for mountains to be moved, and pray that you'll be able to trust God when his answer is "No" or "Not yet." Pray without ceasing, with every breath you have, believing that your sovereign Father loves to give good things to his children.

A Mustard Seed of Faith

Reflect and respond

1. Does your prayer life show that you really believe nothing is impossible for God?
2. Next time God doesn't answer your prayers the way you want, how can you trust that God knows what's best for you? What specific truths about God will you preach to your heart in that moment?
3. James 5:16 tells us that our prayers are powerful and effective. Think of the names of at least three people you love who don't know Jesus personally yet, and commit to faithfully praying for them every single day (maybe for years or decades!) trusting that God is able to do a miracle in their hearts.

Almighty God,
You laid the earth's foundations, and you are the God who can move mountains.
Nothing is impossible for you. Hallelujah!
You reign in heaven and on earth! You have all authority and power!
I exalt your name God!
Forgive me for forgetting to pray, for forgetting to cast all my cares on you.
Forgive me for leaning on my own understanding and trusting in my own strength.
Forgive me for trying to fix problems in my own power instead of running to you.
Forgive me for not trusting your plan, and for doubting your goodness when things don't turn out the way I'd hoped for.
Help me to trust you more.

In Jesus' name,
Amen

Meditation verse for the day:

The prayer of a righteous person is powerful and effective.
(James 5:16)

Day 35

Lessons From Children

(Read Matthew 18:1–9)

A child's humility

Jesus tells his disciples they need to become as lowly as a child in order to enter the kingdom of heaven. Lowly is another word for humble. Jesus is not telling us to act childishly, or suggesting we don't need to mature in our faith. He's saying we need to relate to God in the way a young child relates to her father.

When I take my toddler swimming at the pool, I stand in the deep water and he confidently leaps off the edge towards me. He trusts me with his whole heart. He knows I'm going to catch him and not let anything bad happen to him. He isn't even slightly scared, because his eyes are fixed on mine and his ears are filled with my encouraging voice. He knows very well he can't swim, but he still feels secure and safe. He knows the water is far too deep for him, but he still jumps joyfully and without hesitation. *That* is the humble attitude of a lowly child trusting his loving parent.

All earthly parents are human, so we make mistakes that hurt our children. There are some awful parents who harm their children in terrible ways, intentionally or not. Maybe you have a bad parent who's left you with visible or invisible scars. Maybe you have an absent parent who's disappointed you by never being there when you need them most. You might really struggle to trust God the Father because of how your dad treated you. God wants to heal those deep wounds in your heart.

Psalm 68:5 calls God "a father to the fatherless." God wants to show you that he's the perfect Father you always longed for. He is the trustworthy Father you never had. He'll never let you down. He'll never leave you alone. He's the Father who longs to lavish his overflowing love on you in a way that will build you up and restore your identity. He's the Father who rejoices over you with singing, and who loves to do good for you with all his heart and all his soul. When you jump into his wide-open arms with the trust and humility of a small child, he's delighted to catch you and show you his goodness and his faithfulness. What a God!

If your relationship with your own father is painful, I am so sorry. I strongly suggest talking to a trusted church leader and a Christian therapist about your struggles. Pastor Louie Giglio also has a really powerful book on this exact topic which I highly recommend, called *Not Forsaken: Finding Freedom as Sons and Daughters of a Perfect Father*.

The consequences of sin

Verses 6–9 might seem extreme, because they are. Jesus takes sin extremely seriously, and he's saying we should too. He's not actually telling us to literally chop off parts of our bodies; he is using symbolic exaggeration again to capture our attention and emphasize his point.

Remember how we defined sin, back when we were studying Matthew 3? Sin is *anything* we think or say or do that doesn't put God first, because God deserves to be first in everything. I don't know about you, but a lot of what I think and say and do every moment of every day falls into that category! Just because we sin a lot is no excuse to become comfortable with it, or to just shrug it off and accept it.

We all sin. We also all have pet sins. Pet sins are things we secretly enjoy and don't want to stop doing, even though we know they're wrong. We tell ourselves they aren't really that bad because everyone does them, or that we aren't hurting anybody. Sometimes our culture even tells us to be proud of our pet sins and to celebrate them! Maybe your pet sin is a shopping addiction, greedily wanting more and more and more stuff. Maybe it's lustful daydreams. Maybe it's vanity, and you obsess over every aspect of your appearance all day long. Perhaps your pet sin is idolizing food or sport or money. Maybe you spend your days scrolling through social media coveting other people's lives. Maybe you love to binge-watch TV shows that glorify violence or immorality. You might really enjoy gossiping with your friends, laughing about private details of other people's lives. Perhaps you enjoy holding grudges and feeding anger in your heart, or being very judgmental of others.

Jesus warns us in today's passage that if we're comfortable with our sin, we're on a very dangerous path. We should be running from our sin with all our might, confessing it to the Lord every day and begging him to make our hearts clean and new. We need to always remember that we're fighting a spiritual battle against a powerful and seductive enemy who's trying to destroy us for all eternity.

So what might it look like for you to metaphorically cut off the hand that causes you to sin? You might need to cut off a certain relationship or even get a whole new group of friends. Maybe you need to cut yourself off from social media, or get rid of your internet access altogether. In today's world that's almost unthinkable, but Jesus tells us we should do whatever it takes to choose life with him, no matter how extreme it seems! Imagine if verse 8 said this instead: "If your phone causes you to stumble, throw it away. It is better for you to enter life without a phone than to have a phone and be thrown into eternal fire." It seems radical, but we have to do whatever is necessary to flee the temptations of the devil, who is trying every trick he knows to separate us from God forever. Sin is always serious, because it leads to death.

Reflect and respond

1. *Reflect on the fact that God is our perfect Father. How does that encourage you?*

2. *What sins in your life have you grown too comfortable with? What excuses do you make to yourself for why those sins aren't so bad?*

3. *What extreme actions do you urgently need to take to do battle against your pet sins? How can you prepare yourself to fight or flee next time the temptation arises?*

Lessons From Children

Father God,
I thank you that in your upside-down kingdom, the greatest are those who become humble and dependant like little children.
I thank you that you invite me to trust you with everything that I am.
I praise you are completely trustworthy!
Help me trust you more and more every day.

In Jesus' name,
Amen

Meditation verse for the day:

"They will be my people, I will be their God...
Oh how I'll rejoice in them! Oh how I'll delight
in doing good things for them!"
(Jeremiah 32:38, 41, MSG)

Day 36

Angels and Sheep

(READ MATTHEW 18:10–14)

TODAY LET'S TALK THROUGH another culturally Christian idea: guardian angels. It's really nice to think that God has sent every single one of us a specific guardian angel to protect us, or that our loved ones who have passed away are watching over us from heaven. The problem is that these ideas are not from the Bible. They might sound kind of Christian-y, but they're myths invented by people. Don't be too disappointed though, because what the Bible tells us is so much better.

All about angels

In verse 10, Jesus talks about the angels of his followers being in heaven with God. (Keep in mind that according to verse 6, by "little ones" he's not talking about kids, he means anyone who trusts in him.) Some people use this verse to support the idea of guardian angels, but let's take a quick look through the rest of the Bible's puzzle pieces to see the true big picture about angels.

Hebrews 1:14 tells us that angels are "ministering spirits sent to serve those who will inherit salvation." So not everyone has angels, only Christians. And God sends us these angels so they can serve us. How amazing! Throughout the Bible we see them serving God's people in lots of different ways. They took people like Mary and Joseph messages from God; they looked after Jesus in the desert after he had been tempted by Satan; one helped Peter escape from prison; and they shut the mouths of the hungry lions so that Daniel survived a whole night in their den. One of the most magnificent passages about angels is in 2 King 6, when the prophet Elisha and his servant were surrounded by warriors who were out to capture them. Elisha's servant was scared out of his mind, but then God showed him the hidden spiritual reality of the situation: they were protected by a huge, invisible army of "fiery horses and chariots" (verse 17). How incredible would it have been to see that? Psalm 34:7 tells us that angels are camped around all God's people to protect us. Maybe God will let you catch a glimpse of the angels looking after you one day. Or maybe you'll just have to have faith that his fiery army is protecting you, even when you can't see it or feel it.

Now we know that we don't just have one personal guardian angel always hovering over us. God sends us angels in his wisdom according to our needs: it might be one, or it might be an entire army! But why is Jesus talking about angels in the first place? If we re-read verse 10 for context, we see he's instructing us not to mistreat his beloved followers, because of their angels. The connection between the two things might not be obvious straight away, but Jesus is reminding us how important even the smallest, humblest, weakest disciple is to God. God cares about every single one of us so much he sends his mighty heavenly armies out to protect us. Angels are always before his throne, ready to be sent out to serve us at any moment. We are *that* precious to his heart! So how dare we lead another Christian into sin? How dare we cause them to stumble spiritually as if it's nothing? That person we're showing such disrespect towards is cherished by Almighty God. That person we hate in our hearts is served and protected by God's powerful angels. We need to learn to see each other as God's treasured children, and treat one another as he treats us.

The parable of the wandering sheep

A parable about sheep might seem a bit random here, but remember this is in the context of Jesus talking about his followers — his little ones — who are being led astray into sin. We're all like the wandering sheep in this story. We start out completely lost in our selfishness, but Jesus searches high and low for us until he finds us and welcomes us into his flock. Even once we belong to him, our sinful desires are strong and our willpower is weak. We might let Jesus lead us for a while, happy to trust and follow him, but then we get distracted by a tempting patch of green grass over in the next meadow, so we wander off from the safety of the flock.

The Bible repeatedly uses the metaphor of sheep to represent us, with Jesus as the Good Shepherd who looks after us. It's not a metaphor that makes us look great: sheep are not the most intelligent or capable animals. They can't defend themselves against predators, and they get lost easily. But in Middle Eastern countries in Jesus' day, shepherds protected their sheep with their lives. They fought off lions and wolves with barely any weapons. They lay down across the entrance to the sheep pen at night so their bodies were physically in between their precious sheep and any danger outside. They knew each and every sheep who belonged to their flock, and their sheep knew their shepherd and followed his voice.

How encouraging is it to know that God himself searches for us when we're lost? How stunning is it to think that he cares about every individual one of us, so deeply it's as if we alone are the only one that matters to him? And how incredible is it to know that when the Good Shepherd finds us and brings us home again, he celebrates and rejoices over us? Oh, how he loves us!

Reflect and respond

1. *Think about a Christian you struggle to get on with. How can today's passage about angels change the way you think about them?*
2. *What green-looking 'meadows' have tempted you to wander away from Jesus' flock recently?*
3. *Reflect on Jesus' identity as the Good Shepherd. What does this metaphor show you about his thoughts and feelings towards you?*

Turn in your Bible to Psalm 23.
Pray through it slowly, meditating on who God is, and sharing your gratitude that he's your Good Shepherd.

Meditation verse for the day:

I am the good shepherd. The good shepherd
lays down his life for the sheep.
(John 10:11)

Day 37

Forgiveness

(Read Matthew 18:15–35)

Jesus' teaching on forgiveness can be really hard to accept. Jesus doesn't say here we only have to forgive people who are sorry for what they did. He doesn't say we only need to forgive small sins. He doesn't say we should only forgive people who deserve it. Verse 35 challenges us to see that forgiving others is never optional for Christians. We have to forgive *everyone* who has hurt us, and it has to be true forgiveness from the heart. Sometimes this literally feels like one of the hardest things on earth to do!

The parable of the unmerciful servant

In verse 22, Jesus says we should forgive someone seventy-seven times. Some translations interpret the original text as saying seventy times seven, which is four hundred and ninety times! Now, is Jesus saying that we literally keep count and stop forgiving someone when we get to a very specific number? Of course not; he's speaking metaphorically again. In the Bible, the number seven represents wholeness, so seventy-seven or seven times seven represents boundlessness! Infinite forgiveness! Forgiveness beyond measure!

To illustrate his point Jesus tells the parable of the unmerciful servant. The amount the first servant owes the king — ten thousand bags of gold — is more than he could ever pay back in a thousand lifetimes. It might be like if you owed someone billions of dollars. It's a debt beyond imagining, a debt without a hope of ever possibly being paid. Mercifully, the king cancels this servant's huge debt, saving the man and his family from being jailed or sold into slavery and giving them their lives back. What would you expect the servant's response to be? Rejoicing? A huge feast in celebration? Nope. Instead, this servant immediately sends another man to prison for not repaying a small debt worth about one day's pay.

By telling this parable, Jesus refocuses the whole story of forgiveness on how God treats us. The world teaches us we should forgive others to free ourselves. Jesus says that forgiving others is not actually about us at all. It's all about God. Jesus says all of us have sinned against God our King in the most unimaginably offensive way possible. We've rejected his right to be our Lord. We could try to be righteous for ten thousand lifetimes and never pay off our enormous debt. But God, in his mercy and grace, treats us infinitely better than we ever deserve. He generously forgives all our sins. He pay our debt for us, and in its place he abundantly credits our spiritual bank account with freedom and life and righteousness! Hallelujah!

That's the encouraging part of the story, but next comes the most confronting part. If we receive God's forgiveness but then refuse to forgive people who have hurt us, we're just like the unmerciful servant in the parable. Jesus says we won't be forgiven by God unless we forgive others. Let that sink in for a minute. Scary, isn't it?

Forgiveness is evidence of the Holy Spirit's work

Now Jesus is definitely not saying that we can earn our way into heaven by being really great at forgiving people. There's nothing we can do to earn our salvation — it's a free gift that we don't ever deserve! But he is saying that true Christians are known by their fruit. The ability to forgive others is holy fruit in our lives, evidence we actually belong to God's family. As true Christians, we have the Holy Spirit living inside us, transforming our hearts over time to be like Jesus.

Forgiving people usually goes against everything our hearts tell us is fair and right and just. We want revenge, and we enjoy holding onto grudges. Forgiveness doesn't come naturally to us, but that's actually the point. As Christians we're called to live beyond ourselves. We're being called to be set apart, different. When we're filled with the Holy Spirit, he strengthens us to do things we couldn't dream of doing without him. He empowers us to forgive one another, just as our merciful King has forgiven us. Forgiveness is the proof he's in us. Forgiveness is the evidence our faith is alive. The root of being able to forgive others is a real personal relationship with God. If you're struggling with unforgiveness today, it might be time to take an honest look at your relationship with God first. And take heart! God promises his Holy Spirit to every single Christian. If you're his child, his Spirit already lives in you and you've already been given everything you need to begin learning how to forgive.

What forgiveness looks like

It's really important to look at what the Bible says forgiveness actually is, so that we can also know what it's not. Forgiving someone means:

- We love them and pray for them (Matthew 5:44)
- We do what we can to make peace with them (Romans 12:18)
- We don't seek revenge, but leave justice in God's hands (Romans 12:19)
- We treat them with kindness, understanding and compassion (Luke 6:35; Ephesians 4:32; Romans 12:20)

Forgiving someone doesn't mean we become a doormat, letting them walk all over us and sin against us over and over again. Just because you've forgiven someone doesn't mean you should necessarily trust them again – that might be unwise or even unsafe. Forgiveness doesn't always mean reconciliation. In some situations, we might even need to forgive someone but also cut them out of our lives for good. Forgiving people doesn't mean we're letting them get away without any consequences for their actions. For example, if someone does something illegal against you, you can forgive them and still report them to the police. They should rightfully be punished for their actions, and stopped from mistreating others in the future.

In the same way, God's forgiveness doesn't mean we get to walk away without having to deal with the painful consequences of our sin, such as unplanned pregnancies or broken relationships or getting fired from a job. God often uses these hard experiences to teach us valuable lessons and discipline us, in the way a loving father disciplines his children so they can grow in wisdom and learn from their mistakes.

Reflect and respond

1. What challenges you most from today's devotions? How will it change your perspective and actions in the future?
2. Who do you struggle most to forgive? Why is it so hard to forgive them?

God of mercy,
You're my Creator, and everything I have is a gift from you.
You have every right to reign over every breath I breathe.
Forgive me for trying to run my life my own way.
Thank you for your abundant mercy and grace and forgiveness.
I'm amazed by your goodness to me!
Please help me forgive others the way you forgive me.
I don't want to be like the unmerciful servant.
Please grow the fruit of forgiveness in my life, as evidence to the world that I'm a brand new creation in you.

In Jesus' name,
Amen

Meditation verse for the day:

Be kind and compassionate to one another,
forgiving each other, just as in Christ God forgave you.
(Ephesians 4:32)

Day 38

Marriage

(Read Matthew 19:1–15)

You might be tempted to skim-read or skip over parts of the Bible you don't think apply directly to your life, such as Jesus' words about divorce in today's passage. Don't give in to this temptation. The reason why it's so important to read entire books of the Bible from beginning to end, is that we don't always know what's relevant for us! If we just pick and choose the topics in the Bible we think are important for us to know, we risk missing out on so much of God's message to us. We should still read these passages carefully, praying that God will show us something new about his character and his will for our lives.

The law vs. God's heart

Once again, the Pharisees are trying to stir up controversy with Jesus by asking him a tricky question about when divorce is allowed under Jewish religious law. His response in verse 4 is to point them straight back to Genesis, when God first created marriage. He says marriage is a holy relationship in which a man and a woman are joined together by God, and that humans have no right to break apart that bond. The Pharisees remind Jesus that according to the law God gave Moses, divorce *was* allowed under certain circumstances. Jesus explains that the law was provided because people's sinfulness meant they couldn't handle God's original, holy, perfect plan for marriage.

It's important to clearly explain here that because of the depths of our human brokenness, sometimes divorce is necessary. It breaks God's heart when it happens because it's never good or right or holy, but the Bible doesn't ever encourage people to put themselves in danger by staying in abusive relationships. If you're being abused, you should seek professional help and find a way to leave that situation as quickly and as safely as possible. Eventually you can start to think about forgiving that person, as we learned about in yesterday's passage. But Jesus is not telling you to stay in a relationship that's putting your life or safety at risk.

Preparing properly for marriage

You might feel like it's way too early in your life to be thinking about marriage, let alone divorce and remarriage! But it's always helpful to learn more about God's plan for flourishing human relationships. And knowing how to biblically think about marriage could save you from making some huge mistakes along the way! Jesus' words here show us how seriously God takes marriage. It's a special commitment before God, and his heart's desire is that it lasts for our whole lives. Jesus says that marriage is an unbreakable, sacred union specially designed by God.

So what does that mean for you as a young person? It means that you need to take romantic relationships *very* seriously. The Bible encourages you to guard your heart, and not to awaken love until the time is right (Song of Solomon 8:4). This means you should be very careful who you let yourself develop romantic feelings for. Don't daydream about being in love. Don't be in a rush to find a relationship. Wait for the right person, and then take the time to get to know them really well. Once you let yourself develop feelings for someone, it's very hard to go back.

When you're both young and carefree you might not even think it's a big deal to be married to someone who doesn't love Jesus, but what about when you go through really tough seasons in life? What will happen if one of you gets really sick for a long time? What happens if your child dies? Bad things happen to all of us eventually. How a Christian understands and responds to tragedies is very different to how a non-Christian does, and this will put a huge amount of stress on your relationship. You might find this person sexy or hilarious right now, but deep down do you have the same core values and beliefs? Do they help you love God and your neighbors better? Are they committed to your holiness, building you up into the

MARRIAGE

person God created you to be? Are they passionate about becoming more like Jesus every day?

Carefully study what the Bible teaches about marriage. Pray about it. Talk it through with strong Christian mentors who know you well. You have to make sure your understanding of marriage is shaped by God and not by the culture around you, or your relationship will be in big trouble. A great book to help you along is Timothy Keller's *The Meaning of Marriage*, which looks closely at God's beautiful plan for marriage. Get together with a few close single friends or other young couples to discuss it. Choosing who to marry is literally the second biggest decision you'll ever make in your life, after choosing to become a disciple of Jesus. Choose wisely!

Preparing for singleness

In verses 11–12 Jesus talks about eunuchs. A eunuch is a man who's unable to have sex or ever have children. Jesus says some people are naturally born as eunuchs, others are made this way by surgery, and some people live like eunuchs for God. By this last one, Jesus means some people stay single and choose never to have sex, so that they can commit all of their time and energy to serving God. Jesus says in verse 11 this is a hard life, but that it's given to some people. This shows that a life of singleness and celibacy (which means choosing not to have sex) is sometimes part of God's amazing plan for certain Christians. Jesus himself was single, and he was more perfectly whole than any human has ever been in all of history.

Are you assuming that marriage is the best future God has for you, just because it's what you've always hoped for? Have you ever stopped to wonder whether God has something different in mind for you? Many Christians and churches idolize marriage. Hollywood suggests there's a soulmate out there for each of us, and our society tells us we'll never be truly whole and happy until we get married.

Jesus' words here remind us that for some of us, God's wonderful plan is that we stay single for his glory. So don't build all your hopes and dreams around marriage. Don't write a script in your head for exactly how you think your life should go, because only God knows what's actually best for you. Pray that God will prepare you spiritually for marriage *or* for singleness, and that he'll give you the courage and wisdom to patiently listen to the gentle leading of the Holy Spirit. Learn to find contentment in him alone, knowing that he promises to always be enough for you. That way, you'll be free to follow his unique, special path for your life, whether it leads to marriage or to singleness.

Reflect and respond

1. Who or what are the main influences on how you think about marriage?
2. Why do you think it's so important for Christians to study what God teaches about marriage, instead of learning from movies and pop culture?
3. How has today's devotions changed how you think about your own romantic relationships, both now and in the future?

Lord,
Give me wisdom so I can see love and sex and marriage and singleness as holy gifts from you.
Teach me to have your perspective on these gifts.
I want to follow your will for my life, even if that means my future looks different than I expect.
Prepare me to be content with your plan for me.
Help me to trust you with my future.

In Jesus' name,
Amen

Meditation verse for the day:

So they are no longer two, but one flesh.
Therefore what God has joined together let no one separate.
(Matthew 19:6)

Day 39

The Rich and the Kingdom of God

(Read Matthew 19:16–30)

The rich young man

The young man who Jesus talks with in this passage is a very good person. He's dedicated to obeying God's laws, and he's pretty confident he's doing a great job. He's also really keen to get into heaven, and is checking with Jesus to make sure he's on the right track. Unfortunately for him, his excellent morals and eager attitude are still not enough to save him.

Jesus knows this man's heart and sees that in spite of all his good behavior, money is his most precious treasure, not God. That's why Jesus tells him to give it all away to the poor in verse 21. The young man walks away sadly without doing what Jesus told him, which reveals that his trust and his joy and his identity are in his earthly possessions. The things he owns are his idol. He can't bear to give them away, even if it costs him eternal salvation. Jesus is not out to hurt this man's feelings; he's trying to rescue him by showing him the truth about the deep loves of his heart.

Keep in mind that Jesus is talking to one individual man here, not all humans. He's not saying that all Christians always have to give everything we own to the poor, but he also isn't *not* calling us to do it. Often, Jesus will ask us to give up whatever is holding us back from giving our whole hearts to him. It might be money for one person, romantic relationships for someone else, and a certain lifestyle for another person. We all have different idols to wrestle with. We should each pray urgently that God will reveal our own idols to us, as painful and challenging as it might be to hear. It could be a matter of life or death.

The problem with money

Jesus talks a lot about money and possessions, which tells us it's a really important topic for us to learn and pray about. Some Christians believe money's evil, but the Bible actually tells us "the love of money is a root of all kinds of evil" (1 Timothy 6:10). Money itself is not good or bad, but when we love it too much it causes huge problems in our lives.

In Luke 12:15 Jesus tells a crowd of people to guard their hearts carefully against greed, because life is not about how much stuff we own. Once again, Jesus' values are totally counter-cultural. Our society celebrates materialism, encouraging people to constantly want more and more and more. We live in a world where people get bashed for their expensive sneakers; where countries go to war over natural resources; and where celebrities buy their toddlers cars worth half a million dollars. Companies spend billions of dollars on advertising to make us feel like we'll be left behind if we don't get the newest, biggest, flashiest things. We all casually support modern-day slavery by spending our money on clothes and shoes we don't even really need, even though we know they were made in abusive sweatshops.

We all say money can't buy happiness, but do our actions and thoughts line up with that? The world promises us that money fixes our problems. It promises us that once we have enough we'll finally be free from anxiety and worry, and that we'll feel content and satisfied. It promises that money can give us the respect and admiration of the people around us. It promises us comfort. Security. These promises are all lies. As Ecclesiastes 5:10 tells us, people who love money are never satisfied with what they have, no matter how much they earn. John D. Rockefeller was America's first billionaire and is still considered to have been the richest man in modern history. There's a story of a reporter asking him, "How much money is enough?" His famous reply was, "Just a little bit more." No amount of money or possessions will bring us the joy and contentment our hearts desire. Only God can give us what we're longing for. And the treasure God offers us can't ever get stolen or lost or destroyed, or left behind when we die. He offers us himself.

A biblical approach to money.

The Bible has a lot to say about how to glorify God with our possessions, and it all boils down to this: money is simply a tool that helps us love others. We have to see our possessions as a gift from God to be used for him, in whatever way he calls us to. We can't cling tightly to the things we own, but should be willing to let go of them anytime God gives us an opportunity to use them to care for others. 1 Timothy 6:18 commands us to use our money to "be rich in good deeds, and to be generous and willing to share." Our money is not for us. The earliest Christian churches were made up of both wealthy people and poor people, and Acts 4 tells us they shared everything they had so that no one was ever in need. What a powerfully countercultural way of approaching money! Can you imagine if Christians all over the world were known for radically and generously sharing our money and houses and cars and clothes and technology and food with each other?

That might mean we give everything away to the poor, or it might mean we bless others by randomly sending them a gift-card, or having them over for a meal. Maybe we love our neighbors by paying their bills, or we invite refugees to live in our spare room. I know Christian doctors and dentists who volunteer for a few months every year in poor communities, serving others for free instead of getting paid huge salaries. I know Christians who have given their car away to people who need it more, with no strings attached. Even if you only have a little bit of loose change, you can still occasionally buy a burger for a homeless person.

We don't have to wait until we have a lot of money to be generous – it's not about how much we give, but about why we give or don't give. God isn't honored by the specific dollar amount we give, but by what's in our hearts when we're doing it. He's honored when we remember that everything we have comes from him in the first place. And when we generously and lovingly share our possessions with others and trust God to be enough for us, the world will see that he really *is* our deepest treasure, our identity, our security, and our hope for the future.

Reflect and respond

1. What's your relationship like with money? Do you love it and trust in it more than in Jesus?
2. How can you use the money, possessions, or resources God has given you to love the people around you this week?

God my provider,
You have promised to be everything I need.
Help me to trust in you for my future instead of in my bank account.
Thank you that you're trustworthy and you always keep your promises.
It's so tempting for me to trust in my possessions for my security and my identity and my sense of self-worth.
I want you to be the treasure of my heart, not money.
I want to joyfully use everything you give me to love others in your name.
I want the world to know that you're worth more to me than any amount of money!

In Jesus' name,
Amen

Meditation verse for the day:

Keep your lives free from the love of money
and be content with what you have, because God has said,
"Never will I leave you; never will I forsake you."
(Hebrews 13:5)

Day 40

The Offensive Gospel of Grace

(Read Matthew 20:1–19)

Jesus' parable of the vineyard workers is a simple story with a very deep message. It's a message of hope for each of us, but it can also be a very difficult message to deal with. I have a friend who stopped seeking to get to know Jesus because the message of this story was so offensive to her. Before we study this parable together, take a few moments to pray that God will soften your heart to be able to see his glory in this passage.

Amazing grace

God is represented by the landowner in this parable. He hires people to work in his vineyard at five different times of day. This means that by evening, the first workers have been working hard for over twelve hours. The last people hired would have only worked for a couple of hours, and yet at the end of the day the landowner pays them all the exact same wage. In verse 11, the first group grumble and complain, but the landowner hasn't done anything wrong; he paid them the amount they all agreed on that morning.

Does this situation feel a bit unfair to you? How would you feel if you were in the group hired early in the morning? Annoyed? Jealous? What about if you were one of the last people hired? You'd probably be feeling quite differently! Maybe overwhelmed by the unexpected generosity of the landowner. Probably extremely thankful. And finally, how would you feel if you were the landowner? You might echo his words in verse 15: "Don't I have the right to do what I want with my own money? Or are you envious because I am generous?" How we feel about this story depends a lot on which characters we identify most with.

Jesus tells this parable to show that our God is a God of overflowing abundance and generosity. Just as the landowner enjoys paying people more than they deserve, God delights in freely and radically doing good for us. It brings him joy to shower us with mercy. He doesn't owe us his love, it's a generous gift! There's nothing we could ever do to deserve such grace and mercy. He did it all. Not because we're loveable, but because he is Love. This is the beauty of the gospel! It means that even if we mess up in the worst way possible, we can't lose God's love because we never earned it in the first place. He's given it to us as a free gift, out of the kindness and mercy of his own heart. This is why Christians can have hope and peace. This is why we don't need to feel anxious or be overwhelmed by guilt and shame.

Offensive grace

But here's where it gets really hard. That same grace and mercy we're so thankful to receive freely from God is on offer for everyone. Think about what that actually means. It means that God's forgiveness and love is available for your worst enemy. For that person who bullied you. For that family friend who abused you. For that terrorist who bombed innocent people. For that serial killer who murdered children.

I'll be honest: this idea makes my heart hurt. It feels horrifically unjust. It sometimes makes me question God's wisdom. There are people who are so despicably evil that it feels right they should burn in hell for all eternity. Our spirits yearn for justice to be served.

Let's try to work through why this is such an offensive idea to us by thinking about an extreme example: Hitler. Hitler was responsible for the deaths of six million Jewish people, and at least eleven million others. Imagine if we found out that at the very end of World War II, Hitler repented of his sins and asked Jesus to save him right before he died. How would you feel knowing he'd be in heaven? When you think about it, this is just a much more extreme version of today's parable. We're like the first workers hired, and Hitler is like the last to be hired who receives the same pay as us. It feels like he's getting away with it. It feels like he's being given mercy and grace he doesn't deserve. It feels like God's being horribly unfair.

We'd like to think God would say to him, "Nope, sorry Hitler. You're way too evil for my forgiveness. You don't deserve my mercy. You're going straight to hell!" But we know that when Jesus was on the cross that same kind of scenario happened. Luke 23 tells us that a man on a cross next to Jesus had lived a life of crime, but right before his death he acknowledged his own sin and believed that Jesus was the Son of God. Jesus promised him he would be in heaven that very day. So my guess is that he'd do exactly the same thing for Hitler, as long as Hitler's repentance was real.

My feeling of deep injustice here reveals some things about my own heart that are difficult for me to admit. It shows me that in my pride, I feel like I deserve God's grace and Hitler doesn't. That I feel more entitled to God's forgiveness because my sins aren't as big and obvious. That I feel like there should be a limit to how much evil God forgives. It shows me that I want God's overflowing love and mercy for myself, but not for people who I think have no right to get it. It reveals that I don't really trust God's wisdom, and instead I want to make *myself* the judge of all humanity. I personally want to choose who gets forgiven and who doesn't. But God is saying to me in verse 15, "Don't I have the right to do what I want with my own love and mercy and grace? Or are you envious because I am generous?"

The Bible tells us that every single one of us is completely spiritually dead in our sins, and unable to save ourselves (Ephesians 2:1). None of us deserve salvation. God doesn't owe us a single thing. In fact, all of us deserve justice, which means eternity in hell for not respecting God as God! The Bible tells us that God sent Jesus to die in our place because of how much he loved the whole world (John 3:16). The world that includes me and you, and people like Hitler. The Bible tells us that God is ready to show mercy and forgiveness to *anyone* who genuinely repents and asks God to rescue them from their sin (Psalm 103:11–13). That includes people who are just averagely bad as well as people who are incredibly evil. The Bible tells us that God wants *all* humans to repent and be saved, and that it breaks his heart to think of any of us spending eternity in hell (2 Peter 3:9). And the Bible tells us that God is our Creator and so he has every right to give his mercy to whoever he wants (Romans 9:15).

While it might be really hard for us to process all of that emotionally, we logically can't have it both ways. If God is a God of abundant grace and mercy for me, he's also a God of abundant love for my worst enemy. If God offers forgiveness for every one of my sins, he also offers forgiveness for the sins of the most evil person on earth. He loves lavishing his love on me, and lavishing his love on that person who hurt me so badly. That is how generous our God is. That is how radical the gospel message is.

Reflect and respond

1. What's something from today's devotions that you can be thankful for?
2. What's something from today's devotions that you struggle with, and why?

Wise God,
You are the Creator, and I am your creation.
You are the Shepherd, and I am your little lamb.
You don't owe me anything, but you freely give me everything in Christ Jesus.
Thank you that I can't earn my salvation by being good, so I also can't lose my salvation by being bad.
Help me remember that I'm not more worthy of your love than anyone else.
Forgive me for my pride and self-righteousness.
Help me not to be envious of your radical generosity.
I praise you that you are both a God of justice and a God of mercy.
I thank you that I can trust your wisdom.

In Jesus' name,
Amen

Meditation verse for the day:

"I will have mercy on whom I have mercy,
and I will have compassion on whom I have compassion."
(Romans 9:15)

Day 41

The Greatness of a Servant

(Read Matthew 20:20–34)

In ancient cultures, to sit at the right hand of a king was the highest honor, because the right hand was symbolic of power and authority. So in verse 21, James and John's proud mother is pretty much asking if her sons can be the second most important people in the kingdom of God. That's a pretty bold request! No wonder the other disciples got annoyed about it.

Jesus' response in verse 22 might seem a bit weird if you don't know what cup he's talking about. Throughout the Bible, "the cup" is a metaphor for suffering. When Jesus says that James and John will drink from the same cup as him, he's saying they will have to go through very hard experiences for his sake, suffering the same way Jesus is about to. They've asked for glory and honor, and he explains the path to glory and honor in the kingdom of God is through suffering. That's probably not quite what they were hoping to hear! Keep in mind that Jesus isn't saying all suffering in life necessarily leads to greatness in his kingdom. Just having a hard life is not his point here. He's talking specifically about suffering and being persecuted for our faith, for his sake and the glory of his name.

The counter-cultural kingdom of God

Jesus makes a similarly challenging announcement to the rest of the disciples later, when they're angry at James and John for trying to jump to the front of the line in the kingdom of heaven. They all want positions of honor too! Once again, Jesus' words in verses 25–28 are completely revolutionary and counter-cultural. He says that the path to true greatness in God's eyes is to become a servant to others.

This goes against everything the world teaches us. Society says that to be great you have to be the best. Best at school, best at being creative, best looking, best at making others laugh, best at making money. We get encouraged to only do what feels right to us — to follow our heart — regardless of how it impacts others. We're taught that humility is weakness, that kindness is optional, and that it's our right to put our own desires first in life.

But Jesus tells us that God's kingdom is the exact opposite. To God, lovingly serving others is the most valuable, most worthy way we can spend our lives. There's no culture on earth where servants are the most respected people in their communities. Servants are necessarily seen as being lower in status than the people they serve. Their whole job is about meeting the needs and wants of others. They work in the background, and are usually ignored. They often don't even get thanked or properly appreciated for what they do.

As usual, Jesus is showing us that being his disciple means living very differently to the rest of the world. He's challenging us to be radical in the way we relate to the people around us. Living so counter-culturally doesn't come naturally to us, just like forgiving seventy-seven times, or showing mercy to our enemies, or treasuring God above our own family and friends. When the Holy Spirit lives in us, transforming us to be like Jesus, he teaches us to be servant-hearted. It's more evidence of his work in us. It's more fruit that proves our faith is alive. Holy Spirit-empowered greatness means putting others first in our thoughts and actions out of genuine love for the people God made in his image. God wants us to be characterized by thoughtful, humble, self-sacrificial love for the people around us. Is that how people in your community would describe you?

On a practical level, Jesus doesn't mean we all have to become actual servants. This has nothing to do with our job or position in society, and everything to do with our heart toward others. You can be a senior executive in a Fortune 500 company and still be a servant-leader, known for your kind attitude to your employees, and for putting others' needs before your own. Or maybe you have the intelligence and skills to become a huge success in a respected, high-paying job, but God's given you a passion for a humbler career in service of others. Your own family and friends may feel like you're wasting your potential, or throwing away your future. But the

Bible tells us that all work has dignity and purpose and honor when we do it to the best of our abilities for God (Colossians 3:23). Whether we clean toilets or run companies or flip burgers or do brain surgeries or stay at home raising children, we can all achieve greatness by lovingly serving the people around us. God's idea of success looks very, very different than the world's idea of success. Whose version of success are you aspiring to?

The Son of Man came to serve

Jesus was the perfect role model of this type of greatness. But we'd be missing the central part of the story if we only saw Jesus as a good role model here. He is an example to us, but he's also so much more. As Pastor Tim Keller regularly says, "The gospel is good news, not good advice."[1] Advice tells us what *we* need to do. News tells us what God has already done *for us*. The good news is that Jesus came to earth to serve us. The good news is that the God who handcrafted every fish in the ocean humbled himself to serve us. The good news is that the God who designed the petals of every stunning flower in every field hung on that cross to serve us. That's the good news of the gospel. It's almost unimaginable that he would sacrifice himself like that out of love for us. It makes no sense! What a God!

In John 13, Jesus serves his disciples by washing their feet. Peter's upset that his beloved master would do such a humble, dirty job and refuses to let him, but Jesus says, "Unless I wash you, you have no part with me" (verse 8). He's showing Peter that not asking Jesus to help us is a sign of pride. Not allowing Jesus to serve us means he is not our Savior. We can't wash ourselves clean. We can't save ourselves. We need to accept his help. We need to cry out for rescue to a Father who delights in gently, lovingly serving his children and meeting our deepest needs at his own expense.

---

1. Keller, *Hidden Christmas*, 21.

Reflect and respond

1. Jesus says the path to greatness in his kingdom is through suffering and sacrificing for him. How does this impact the way you think about your life?
2. Meditate on all the ways that Jesus humbled himself to serve us. What does that mean to you personally? How does it make you feel? Express your gratitude out loud!

Heavenly Father,
Thank you for the good news of the gospel.
Thank you that Jesus came to serve and save lost sheep like me.
I praise you that he sacrificed himself out of love for me.
I can't thank you enough! I love you!
Teach me how to be a humble servant like Jesus.
Help me love other people with your radical, selfless love.

In Jesus' name,
Amen

Meditation verse for the day:

Whoever wants to become great among you must be your servant . . . just as the Son of Man did not come to be served, but to serve, and to give his life as a ransom for many.
(Matthew 20:26, 28)

Day 42

Jesus the King

(Read Matthew 21:1–27)

The humble King

Today's passage opens with Jesus' entrance into Jerusalem, exactly one week before Easter Sunday. Christians celebrate this day as Palm Sunday. Jesus has less than a week to go until he's crucified, and he knows it. Interestingly, time seems to slow down at this point in all four Gospels. We get way more information on this one week of Jesus' life than on his first thirty years! That's because he's getting closer and closer to his ultimate goal: the cross. This is what it's all been about, and where his life and ministry were always heading. In this single passage, three different Old Testament prophecies are fulfilled, which is more than usual! This is because Jesus is ramping things up, revealing who he really is to anyone who's willing to listen. In these important final days, he's showing that he *is* the Messiah they've been waiting for. He is the one who the prophets spoke of. He is the Savior of the world! He's finally come, and is ready to take his place as King.

Jerusalem was an ancient city which became the Israelite's capital under King David. His son Solomon built God's temple there, which made it a special place for Jewish people both historically and spiritually. Jesus the King doesn't enter this important city on a warrior's magnificent warhorse, but on a borrowed donkey that's not even fully grown. He isn't surrounded by an army of soldiers, but by a group of ordinary fishermen. He's gentle and slow, trotting along on his humble little animal. The parallel version of this story in Luke 19 tells us Jesus is so broken-hearted he even cries as he rides along. And yet a very large crowd of people respond to his arrival by spreading their cloaks and palm branches along the road, shouting out their praise. In the Old Testament, this is the way they celebrated a new king being crowned.

But what were these people expecting from Jesus? Most probably hoped he was finally here to lead the Jewish people in a battle against the Romans for their freedom. They expected the Christ to overthrow their oppressors and bring in a new era of independence and glory for the Jewish nation. No one would have expected that for Jesus, becoming king meant he would give up his life that very week.

The temple

In verse 12 Jesus heads for the holiest place in the city: the temple. This is the exact place from Luke 2, where he hung out for days on end when he was only twelve years old, enthusiastically talking with the rabbis about God. It's obviously a special place for him, his Father's house. It's the week of the Jewish celebration of Passover, so the city is filled with hundreds of thousands of Jewish people who have travelled from all over the countryside, and the temple is absolutely packed! At Passover, Jewish families remember how God rescued them from slavery in Egypt. Some families bring animals with them to sacrifice, while others buy animals once they get to the temple. That's why the temple court is like a busy marketplace when Jesus walks in that day, filled with animals for sale and moneychangers, who are exchanging currencies for people who had travelled from out of town, so they could pay the temple taxes.

Verse 12 ends really dramatically. It's quite shocking to imagine our gentle, meek Jesus, suddenly turning over tables and flipping chairs! In fact, this isn't even the first time he's done it. As a devout Jewish man, Jesus had been coming to the temple on Passover every single year of his life, and John 2 describes him at the very start of his public ministry, making a whip and forcing everyone out of the temple court. So what on earth is going on here?

Jesus is furious that God's temple — which should be a sacred place of prayer and worship — is being used by people to make money. In verse 13 he calls it a "den of robbers" so we know customers are being ripped off. The fact that Matthew 21 and John 2 both specifically mention the dove sellers is also really important. Doves were sold to poor people who couldn't afford to sacrifice a bigger animal. This tiny detail shows us Jesus was particularly upset that poor people were being taken advantage of.

God's wrath

You might be wondering how the Bible can say Jesus never sinned, when in this situation he's so angry that he's flipping over tables! Jesus' anger in this situation is a righteous, holy anger. It isn't sinful anger at all. He's right to be angry! He is *so* passionate about his Father's glory, and is rightfully upset that God is being dishonored in his own temple. He hates evil with such a burning passion, that it makes him furious to see it happening in this holy place. He loves his children so deeply, that it enrages him to witness poor people being taken advantage of as they come to worship God.

The Bible actually talks a lot about God's wrath, which is another word for his anger. It tells us that God is very patient and is slow to become angry, but not that he *never* gets angry. Theologian J. I. Packer explains that God is never angry in the sinful ways that humans get angry, where we lose our temper or our self-control, over-reacting and lashing out because we feel hurt or attacked. The Bible only ever describes God being angry as "a right and necessary reaction to objective moral evil. God is only angry where anger is called for."[1] As a perfectly holy God, he hates sin, and it breaks his heart. As a perfectly loving God, he hates anything that ruins his creation and hurts his people. If God didn't feel anger at sin, wouldn't we question whether or not he is truly good and just? If he didn't get angry at the bad things that hurt us so deeply, wouldn't we question whether or not he truly loves us? None of us want a God who just shrugs his shoulders and looks the other way when evil happens. His holy anger towards sin is a result of his heart for justice. It's evidence of his love.

Reflect and respond

1. *What makes you angry? Do you get angry at the same things as God does? Or is your anger usually self-centered and sinful?*
2. *How can thinking about God's righteous anger toward evil lead you to worship him?*

---

1. Packer, *Knowing God*, 170.

Holy God,
You are perfect in righteousness and purity and justice.
I praise you that you hate evil, and death, and pain, and suffering.
Help me not to avoid parts of the Bible that make me feel uncomfortable,
like the parts that talk about your anger.
I want to know you for who you really are, not just for who I'd like you to be.
Help me to love what you love, and to hate what you hate.

In Jesus' name,
Amen

Meditation verse for the day:

The wrath of God is being revealed from heaven
against all the godlessness and wickedness of people.
(Romans 1:18)

Day 43

Warnings for the Self-Righteous

(READ MATTHEW 21:28–46)

JESUS TELLS THESE TWO parables as a strong warning to the chief priests and the Pharisees. It's easy to imagine that they were bad people who obviously deserved Jesus' harsh words, but remember that these were most respected religious leaders in the community. On the outside they seemed to be very holy people. That means there's also a warning in these parables for any of us who consider ourselves to be pretty good Christians.

The parable of the two sons

Jesus' first parable describes two sons who respond in opposite ways to their father. The father represents God. The first son ignores his father to begin with, but eventually goes and helps in the family vineyard. Jesus says that this son represents sinners like tax collectors and prostitutes. These are people who know without a doubt that their hearts and lives are a mess. They're hurting and lost and alone, and know that they're stuck in sin. They can't fix what's broken inside them on their own, so they run to God in repentance and trust him to rescue them.

The other son promises to help out in the family vineyard but then doesn't end up actually doing it. He represents outwardly religious people like the chief priests and Pharisees. These are the people who say they believe in God and might even follow God's laws really well, but their identity and sense of self-worth really comes from being moral. They idolize being good. They don't really feel like they have much to repent for. They might never say it out loud, but they think they're fine on their own without really needing God's forgiveness and grace and mercy. They look down on 'sinners' and judge others, believing in their hearts they're better than the people around them.

Jesus warns his audience (and us!) that it's the repenting sinners who'll end up in heaven, not the good religious folk. What we say we believe doesn't matter to God, it's our heart that counts. It's where we practically put our trust that really matters.

The parable of the tenants

Jesus' second parable in verse 33 makes the same point again, but in a different way. He describes a vineyard that's been rented out to some farmers. The landowner represents God, and the renters represent the religious leaders. The servants he sends to collect the harvest symbolize the prophets who came to warn the people to repent, like John the Baptist. Jesus is the vineyard owner's son, who gets killed by the renters.

Jesus is helping us see that God has every right to judge humanity — after all, he owns the whole vineyard! All of creation is his. But this parable also shows that God graciously gives people plenty of chances to respond rightly to him. He sends prophet after prophet and servant after servant to get his message across, waiting patiently for people to treat him as God. Jesus warns us that in the end, salvation won't belong to the people who shamelessly respond with arrogance and pride. It won't belong to the people who try to live life on their own terms by acting like the vineyard belongs to them. The opportunity to be saved will be given to people who respond to God the way he rightfully deserves. People who humbly bear God-honoring fruit, proving that they've repented by the way they live.

It might seem really harsh for Jesus to talk about crushing the enemies of God like he does in verse 44, but that's the ultimate reality of rejecting God. Revelation 5 describes Jesus as both the Lamb and the Lion. At this point in history, we mainly experience him as the Lamb. He's our gentle, servant-hearted Savior, who rode into Jerusalem weeping on the back of a small donkey. But he's also the Lion, and soon we'll experience the terrible, awesome fullness of what that means. He'll ride in from the clouds on a majestic white horse, followed by all the armies of heaven. He'll be crowned King of kings and Lord of lords, and he'll judge us all from his throne. He'll wage one final war against everyone who's rejected his free gift of righteousness, throwing them into the eternal fires of hell (Revelation 19). Our God is slow to anger, but he hates sin and he *will* judge it one day. Our God is patient and gives us chance after chance after chance to respond to him in humble repentance, but his patience won't last forever. Don't miss your chance.

Our personal response to these parables

In both these parables, Jesus is saying that every single person needs to repent and turn back to God, not just the people we think of as being particularly bad. Not one of us can stand before God on Judgment Day and say that we're worthy of God's forgiveness; we need Jesus' righteousness covering us. Tim Keller suggests some helpful questions we can ask ourselves to check if we're like the self-righteous religious leaders, which I've paraphrased here:

1. Do you know that you're a hopeless sinner? Do you agree that God has every right to throw you into hell right this minute because of how messed up your heart is?

2. Do you look around you at the way others live and judge them in your heart? Or do you think: *My heart is sinful just like theirs; it just shows itself differently in my life.*[1]

The good news is that no matter how you answered those questions today, if you're broken-hearted about your sin and know you can't rescue yourself, Jesus is ready and waiting for you with open arms. Surrender to him, and be welcomed joyfully into the family of God.

Reflect and respond

1. *What did your responses to the two reflection questions show you about your heart? Are you more like the Pharisees or the humble 'sinners'?*

2. *How do you feel when you think about standing alone before the throne of the King of kings on Judgment Day? Why does it make you feel that way?*

3. *What does today's devotions lead you to worship God for?*

---

1. Keller, *Romans 1–7*, 44.

Most High God,
Thank you for sending Jesus as a humble, compassionate, servant-leader.
Thank you for your patience in not throwing all evil into hell yet, but generously waiting so that more people have a chance to repent and turn to you.
Thank you for your kindness and mercy in saving me, a helpless sinner.
Please show me all the ways I'm like the Pharisees.
Please search my heart and reveal my self-righteousness.
Help me see the ways I'm trusting myself instead of you.
Give me faith in you alone.

In Jesus' name,
Amen

Meditation verse for the day:

Therefore I tell you that the kingdom of God will be taken away from you and given to a people who will produce its fruit.
(Matthew 21:43)

Day 44

The Wedding Banquet – Part 1

(Read Matthew 22:1–14)

This parable is really similar to the two we read yesterday, and Jesus is still talking to the same religious leaders. He's repeating himself because he obviously wants to make a very clear point, emphasizing the same idea in three different ways. If this message is so important to him, we'd be wise to listen carefully to his words. We're actually going to slow right down and take two days to study this one parable, because there is just so much to learn from it!

A joyful celebration of great abundance

When a king throws a banquet to celebrate his son's wedding, it's a spectacular event. He prepares all the very best foods possible and spares no expense. Some of us have this idea that heaven is just going to involve lounging around on clouds playing harps, surrounded by boring people. Nope! Heaven is going to be like a magnificently generous feast, an eternal celebration of Love, a loud party filled with joy and laughter!

The distractions of this life

And yet in verse 5, the first group of guests have a bizarre reaction to the invitation to this luxurious banquet: they refuse to come! Who would reject such a wonderful offer from a powerful king? Some of them even wander off to deal with everyday concerns like work. Now, taking your responsibilities seriously and working hard are good things that we all should do in life, but if they come before God in our hearts then we have a deadly spiritual problem. We can honor God with our work or we can idolize our work. It's not the work that's the problem, it's our attitude towards it. You might think that if you were in their place you wouldn't have just gone back to work instead of attending the party of a lifetime, but in reality but we all regularly do the exact same thing.

We plan to read our Bibles, but we have things that urgently need to be done so we never get around to it. We want to pray, but we get caught up doing a bunch of errands and it just slips our mind. We mean to spend quality time with God, but we don't put it at the top of our list so it just never ends up happening. We get so caught up in the ordinary cares of daily life, that we hardly even notice we've missed our invitation to have a personal relationship with God until it's too late.

There are so many wonderful things that God made for us to enjoy in this world. He wants us to build beautiful relationships with each other. He wants us to work and be productive and creative. He wants us to take pleasure in music and nature and our achievements. But we tend to focus so much on enjoying these little everyday pleasures that we forget about the One who gave them to us as a loving gift. That act of forgetting and focusing on the gift instead of the Giver is extremely disrespectful to God. We should be enjoying these gifts with a heart filled with awe and gratitude, thankful that we have such a generous Father!

C. S. Lewis described the way we get our priorities all mixed up like this:

> "We are half-hearted creatures, fooling about with drink and sex and ambition when infinite joy is offered us, like an ignorant child who wants to go on making mud pies in a slum because he cannot imagine what is meant by the offer of a holiday at the sea. We are far too easily pleased."[1]

Like the little child Lewis talks about, we think living life our own way is the greatest fun we could ever have. We can't even begin to imagine the vast freedom and beauty of walking with God and discovering who he made us to be. We're often so busy enjoying God's earthly gifts that we don't even realize we're missing out on the invitation to experience a much greater joy.

---

1. Lewis, *Weight of Glory*, 2.

The king's rage

Read verse 7 again. It is a hard verse to hear. We've spent so much time lately reading about the gentle, merciful love of God, that it's difficult to think he's the same God who will completely destroy people on Judgment Day. But we can't pick and choose the parts of God we like and ignore the other parts. If we do that, we're inventing our own imaginary god who thinks and acts just like us. We're making up a personalized religion based on what makes us feel comfortable. We're suggesting that we would be a better god than God.

Our God is a God of love and mercy, *and* of righteousness and justice. Because he is absolutely holy, he has to punish sin. He can't just ignore it, or he wouldn't be just anymore. We might all have different standards about what right and wrong are, but we agree in our hearts that people who do bad things should be punished. None of us want violent criminals walking free, or evil dictators living happily ever after on their piles of money. Our spirits yearn for justice every time we watch the daily news, or whenever someone hurts us.

But we want God to bring his eternal justice down on *other* people, more evil people. We tend to think hell is a bit of an overreaction for normal, decent people like us. But where's the line? And who gets to choose where the line is? Should murderers go to hell but liars get into heaven? Should racists go to hell but greedy people get into heaven? God says that as our Creator, only he has the right to choose. And he draws a very simple, clear line. He says that the line is between those who reject his lordship and those who submit to him. And we *all* rebel against his right to be our King. Some of us do it in big ways and some in small, but all of us do it, so he has every right to punish us for it. All of us. But because he's a God of love and mercy he gives us a way out. He offers to accept the punishment on our behalf, so that justice is still served. He's patiently holding off on Judgment Day for a while, giving people a chance to get their banquet invitation and decide how to respond to it. Just remember, God's wrath is real and he will not be patient forever.

Reflect and respond

1. What things are taking up your time and emotions right now, distracting you from your relationship with God and threatening your place at the eternal wedding feast?
2. Reflect on all of the good earthly gifts that God your loving Father has generously gifted to you for you to enjoy. How can you practice being grateful to God this week?

Dear Lord,
Thank you for inviting me to spend eternity in heaven with you.
Thank you that I can't even imagine how incredible it will be.
I forget that this world isn't my home, heaven is.
Help me not to waste my life on things that won't last.
Thank you so much for all the wonderful gifts you've given me to enjoy!
Thank you that you delight in being my provider and my generous Father.
Forgive me for enjoying your gifts more than I enjoy you.
Teach me how to love you more.
I want you to be my only treasure.
Set my heart on you.

In Jesus' name,
Amen

Meditation verse for the day:

No one's ever seen or heard anything like this,
never so much as imagined anything quite like it –
what God has arranged for those who love him.
(1 Corinthians 2:9, MSG)

Day 45

The Wedding Banquet — Part 2

(Read Matthew 22:1-14)

BOTH OF THE FIRST two parables in chapter 21 involved the offer of salvation being taken off one group and given to others instead. The exact same thing happens here. The king has a wedding hall full of amazing food but no guests! So he sends out his servants to bring in anyone they can find on the street corners. Everyone is welcome to this banquet. This reminds us that heaven is on offer for anyone. It doesn't matter what's happened in your past. It doesn't matter if you're intelligent or not, attractive or not, rich or not. It doesn't matter if you're a nice person or a terrible person. The King of kings is extending a wonderful invitation to all of us, an exclusive opportunity to attend the only party that matters in life.

So far, this parable is very similar to the two that came before it, but in verse 11 Jesus adds an important twist. The invitation says everyone's welcome, but there's just one catch: *to come, you have to be wearing the right clothes*. If we get caught at the wedding feast in our own casual, everyday clothes, we'll be tied up and kicked out of the eternal party into eternal sadness. But what does this metaphor actually mean? How do we know what the 'right clothes' are? And how do we make sure we're wearing them?

Wedding clothes

The Bible uses the metaphor of clothes a lot, to represent how God sees us. What he sees when he looks at us will decide whether we belong at that banquet table or not. Thankfully, our generous Father doesn't want us to go on some kind of self-improvement program. It's not at all about trying harder to be a better person so that we deserve our seat at the table. In fact, people who just try harder to be good are the ones who show up to the banquet in what the Bible calls the "filthy rags" of self-righteousness (Isaiah 64:6).

Self-righteous people say in their hearts, "I deserve to be here because I'm actually pretty good. I'm not a bad person, so God owes me a seat at his banquet." God is offended when we try to 'wear' our own righteousness to the wedding feast. It's prideful and arrogant and it will never be good enough for our perfectly holy God. We will never be well-dressed enough for his luxurious banquet! We all sin. We all fall short of what's required. Even our best efforts can never be more than dirty rags compared with what God is worthy of.

So if it isn't about trying really hard to be better people, how do we find clothes to wear to the banquet? God himself actually graciously provides us with the perfect wedding clothes, as a gift. When we humbly accept his banquet invitation, acknowledging that we don't have anything of our own that's good enough to wear, an incredible switch takes place. Jesus wears our sin and shame and brokenness and gives us his own perfect holiness to wear instead. God personally takes off our disgusting rags and wraps us up in the shining robe of Jesus' perfect righteousness (Isaiah 61:10). That means that on Judgment Day when God looks at me all he sees is Jesus' righteousness, not all my sin. What an incredible exchange!

The gospel

In this parable, Jesus is once again giving us an incredible picture of the gospel message. He reminds us that our heavenly Father adores us and wants us all at his glorious heavenly banquet, even though we haven't done a single thing to deserve it. God lovingly searches all the corners of earth to find us, to make sure we get our invitation. We can receive his invitation no matter who we are or what we've done. Our responsibility is to choose how we'll respond to his invitation. But once we accept, we can't just come to the party any way we like. That's arrogant and disrespectful to our King, and it's *his* party. We have to humbly accept the perfectly clean, new wedding clothes the King gives us to wear. We have to let Jesus trade our dirty rags for his shining white robe. We have to accept God's offer to make us a new creation.

The Wedding Banquet — Part 2

It's worth taking the time today to reflect on which clothes you're planning to wear to the wedding banquet. We don't know when the end will come, and we need to be ready. We have to make sure we aren't trusting in our own righteousness to please God. We have to make sure we're humbly clothed in Jesus' righteousness alone, so we don't get kicked out of the feast. It's actually the most important thing in life.

Reflect and respond

1. *Imagine you're standing before God's throne at the end of your life, and he asks you why you deserve to be allowed into his wedding feast. What will your answer be?*
2. *What part of God's nature has this parable helped you see or appreciate more?*

God of heaven,
You have searched for me and invited me home.
You have removed my sins from me, as far as the east is from the west.
You have clothed me in Jesus' perfect righteousness.
You have filled me with the same Spirit who raised Jesus from the dead, so that I can have a brand new life.
And it's all completely free and completely undeserved.
All I have to do is accept your invitation, and rely on you for my salvation.
Thank you, thank you, thank you!
You are worthy of all praise Lord.

In Jesus' name,
Amen

Meditation verse for the day:

For it is by grace you have been saved, through faith —
and this is not from yourselves, it is a gift from God —
not by works, so that no one can boast.
(Ephesians 2:8–9)

Day 46

The Greatest Commandment — Part 1

(READ MATTHEW 22:15–46)

IN THE REST OF chapter 22 we see the religious leaders getting together to try and trap Jesus by asking him controversial questions. They're looking for any excuse to turn the crowds against him or get him arrested. He knows exactly what they're doing, and responds calmly, with self-restraint and wisdom. In spite of themselves they end up amazed by him!

In the middle of all this, Jesus says a small sentence that should revolutionize your entire existence. In verse 37 he says that the most important thing for anyone to do with their life is this: "Love the Lord your God with all your heart and with all your soul and with all your mind." Since he says this should be the number one priority of our *whole entire lives*, let's take some time over the next few days to slow down and explore exactly what it means.

Love

I'll never forget the first time I heard someone praying say, "I love you!" to God. I was used to people praising God, thanking God, or asking God for things. But hearing someone simply express their love for God changed everything for me. Some of us follow Jesus because it's just how we were raised. Some of us follow Jesus out of fear of going to hell. Some of us follow

Jesus because it feels comfortable and familiar to us, or because we're looking for a sense of security in this crazy world. There are a thousand reasons why people follow Jesus. But how many of us follow Jesus because we cherish him? Because we find him breath-takingly beautiful? Because being in his presence brings us deep delight? Because we just couldn't imagine living a moment without him? Ask yourself right now: do I actually *love* God?

"All"

The language used in this command is not half-hearted. The word 'all' is repeated three times, so Jesus obviously means it. 'All' means everything, all the time, in every way. It's undeniably, unmistakably extreme. We are to give him all our allegiance and loyalty. He wants us to be all in for him. It's an exclusive relationship: we can't have more than one first love. We can't sing praises to God on Sunday mornings but then forget he exists the rest of the week. God wants all of me and all of you, all the time, to be all for him.

Our hearts

The first thing we're commanded to love God with is our hearts. Pastor Dane Ortlund explains: "The heart, in biblical terms, is not part of who we are but the center of who we are. Our heart is what defines and directs us."[1] This means that God is to have the first place in our desires, our passions, our motivations, and our emotions. We're to find our deepest joy in him, and to enjoy and delight in him more than we do in anything else. We should feel like we can't get enough of him, like we're always hungry for more. We should look forward to our time with him. Our spirits should sing when we think of him. Sometimes we fall into the trap of thinking that our main responsibility as Christians is to do work for God, serving in church and sharing the gospel. But actually, our main responsibility is to adore who God is! Everything else in life flows from there.

But how?

But what if we don't delight in God? How do we learn to enjoy him more? Is it just about trying harder? Can we force our hearts to love him? Fortunately, as a follower of Jesus the solution never comes from our own strength

---

1. Ortlund, *Gentle and Lowly*, 18.

and willpower. All the way through the Bible we see God asking us to obey him, and then promising that he'll help us be able to obey him. When we come to him humbly on our knees, his Spirit helps us understand and love him more. That way it's always God who gets the glory in our lives. That way none of the pressure is on us to try and do better, and being a Christian doesn't become just another self-help program.

All through the Old Testament there are examples of God promising his people that if they turn back to him in humble repentance, he'll give them a new heart, he'll cleanse their hearts, he'll soften their hearts, and he'll write his law on their hearts (Ezekiel 36:26; Jeremiah 31:33). Our sin makes us so self-centered, that we can't help but put ourselves at the center of our own hearts and lives. But when we admit that to God, and ask for his forgiveness and his help, he can't wait to give it to us. He delights to provide for his children. He is Love, and he is longing to put his love in our hearts.

That doesn't mean that we just sit back and relax though! Just like in human relationships, we can't really love someone properly until we get to know them. We might like how they look or admire their reputation, but deep love grows over many years as we invest our time in getting to know who they really are at the deepest level. We have to be disciplined and prioritize making time to know God better every day. As we learn about who he is and focus on what he's done throughout the history of the world, we'll start to find him more and more beautiful. As he reveals his glory to us through the Bible, we'll be more and more astonished and amazed by him. As his Holy Spirit renews our hearts, we will start to treasure him more and enjoy him more deeply.

Reflect and respond

1. *What would have to change in your life for God to be your first love, and for you to find your satisfaction in him alone?*
2. *Where have you seen God's beauty and majesty this week?*

Open your Bible to Psalm 63 and pray slowly through the first 8 verses. This psalm is the stunning cry of a human being who desperately loves God with his whole heart. Ask God to make each verse true of your own relationship with him.

The Greatest Commandment — Part 1

Meditation verse for the day:

I love you, Lord, my strength.
(Psalm 18:1)

Day 47

The Greatest Commandment — Part 2

(Read Matthew 22:34-40)

What is the soul?

IN HIS NOVEL *Klara and the Sun*, the brilliant writer Kazuo Ishiguro deals with the idea of souls. His story explores whether a very intelligent AI robot could ever learn to understand an individual human well enough to really *become* them, continuing on life as them once they die, or whether there's something special about each human that can't ever be copied and transferred into another being. What do you think? If you died, could a robot take your place by looking and talking and walking and thinking and responding and feeling and making decisions just like you? Would your loved ones be able to relate to that robot as if it was really and truly *you*? Could a robot ever be you in your entirety? What would be the difference?

While philosophers have debated exactly how to define souls for centuries, we all know that human beings are much more than just physical bodies. We sense that the moment a person dies, something essential to who they are is gone from their body. The Bible, which often uses the words 'soul' and 'spirit' to mean the same thing, teaches us that our soul is the part of us that will continue to exist for all eternity. Our soul is our deepest self, our inner being, our unique essence. It's the spiritual part of us that makes us who we are. Our soul is what Jesus saved on the cross, and it's what the Holy Spirit transforms over time as we grow more spiritually mature. It's the part of us that leaves our body when we die. It's also the part of us that God promises will be given a perfect, new heavenly body for all eternity.

Jesus tells us in today's passage that we should love God with our whole soul. This means that every part of our being should be built around our love for him. He comes first in what makes us who we are. He is the foundation of our *us-ness*, the ground that our roots are growing in, the heartbeat of our lives, the soundtrack to our story. He's the lens we see the whole of existence through, and he's the reason we think and act and believe and feel the way we do. He shapes our understanding of ourselves and the people around us. All of who we are should joyfully proclaim, "Jesus is Lord!"

The work of the Holy Spirit

Because the soul is such a tricky thing to define, it can be callenging to work out how to practically love God with all our soul. How do we actually put him at the center of our being? The Bible tells us there are two parts to it. The first part is through the supernatural working of the Holy Spirit in us. God promises that all his children have been given the Holy Spirit, who puts his love inside us. Paul's prayer in Ephesians 3:16–19 is incredibly beautiful and powerful:

> "I pray that out of his glorious riches he may strengthen you with power through his Spirit in your inner being, so that Christ may dwell in your hearts through faith. And I pray that you, being rooted and established in love, may have power, together with all the Lord's holy people, to grasp how wide and long and high and deep is the love of Christ, and to know this love that surpasses knowledge – that you may be filled to the measure of all the fullness of God."

This is a soul-transforming prayer. It should be the cry of our hearts every single day, if we truly want to love God with all our soul. We should long for the Holy Spirit to live in us and strengthen our inner being – which is our soul – giving us faith. We should pray believing that the Holy Spirit can and will root our souls firmly in the love of God, so that all of the rest of our life is like a beautifully lush garden growing up out of that rich, healthy soil, flourishing and blossoming and thriving. We should pray for God's Spirit to open our eyes to just how deeply and truly he loves us. We want to *know* his love for us in a way that goes far beyond just head-knowledge. We want to feel it, to experience it, and to live it. We don't just want to read about his love in the pages of the Bible, we want to taste and see it for ourselves. We want his love to be the deepest, truest reality of our existence. We need his love to be at the very center of our being. And we should pray that as the Holy Spirit strengthens and teaches our soul, we will be filled with all the fullness of God himself. I can't even begin to imagine what that might mean, but just thinking about it brings me to my knees.

God offers us himself in all his fullness. An abundance of God. He's not holding back. Don't settle for a half-hearted, luke-warm faith that doesn't really impact who you are at the deepest level. Don't be content with a faith that isn't basking in God's endless love for you, and that isn't radiant with love back toward him. Pray desperately for more of God. Pray for the Holy Spirit to set your eternal soul on fire for God. Pray for your inner being to be filled to overflowing with all the fullness of Almighty God. Beg for his love to take root and grow inside you. Depend on him for it. Seek it with all your heart. He loves to give himself to his children, and he wants to give you the gift of his love in your soul.

Our responsibility

The second part of loving God with all our soul is our own personal responsibility. In Deuteronomy 4:9 Moses says, "Only take care, and keep your souls diligently, lest you forget the things that your eyes have seen, and lest they depart from your heart all the days of your life. Make them known to your children and your children's children" (ESV). Moses is warning the Israelites that they have to be very careful to constantly remember who God is and what he's done for them. 'Keep your soul' means to guard it and protect it, keeping it for God alone. We are forgetful people. We get distracted and side-tracked. Being diligent about remembering God means to be disciplined and intentional about keeping him at the front of our minds. We should constantly talk about him with our Christian community, regularly celebrating his goodness together. We should sing songs that remind us of his character and retell the stories of his love to us. We should memorize Scripture and teach it to our children and grandchildren. This is how we guard our souls, and cultivate spirits that remain rooted in love for God.

Psalm 63:1–2 beautifully shows us what it looks like to deliberately nurture a love for God in our souls:

> "O God, you are my God, earnestly I seek you;
> my soul thirsts for you; my flesh faints for you,
> as in a dry and weary land where there is no water.
> So I have looked upon you in the sanctuary,
> beholding your power and glory.

David's soul is desperate for more of God. He's refusing to be satisfied by anything less than God. So what does he do? He seeks God earnestly, which means he's very focused and serious about it. He turns his gaze toward God's heavenly throne. He fixes all his attention on who God is. He beholds God's power and glory, drinking it in, marvelling at it. How do we do this in our own lives? We prioritize spending time with God each day because we long to soak in his presence. We pore over the Bible, yearning to see new glimpses of his majesty. We diligently study what he's revealed about himself in his Word, growing in our adoration and wonder at his power and glory. We sing his praises every chance we get, reflecting on his character and his love towards us. And we pray our way through our days, sharing our deepest self with him in honesty and vulnerability.

Reflect and respond

1. *What's something that really encouraged you from today's devotions?*
2. *What's something that really challenged you from today's devotions?*

Living God,
Be my everything.
Be my center.
I want to be so in love with you that the whole world can tell.
I want the truest things about me to be that I am loved by you, and that I love you.
I want to be wholly yours.
I surrender everything I am to you.

In Jesus' name,
Amen

Meditation verse for the day:

Praise the Lord, my soul;
all my inmost being, praise his holy name.
(Psalm 103:1)

Day 48

The Greatest Commandment — Part 3

(READ MATTHEW 22:34-40)

Engaging our minds

Today we'll start exploring what it means to love God with our minds. Jesus doesn't call his followers to just blindly believe in him without engaging our brains. God is big enough to handle any doubts and questions we have. He wants us to fully engage our ability to think, and to wrestle thoughtfully with the hard stuff we read in the Bible. He gave us all unique brains that process information in different ways, and we understand things from a variety of perspectives. This means that when we use our minds to love God in a church community with other Christians, we can share fresh insights with one another and have our own understanding stretched and broadened and challenged!

Jesus also doesn't want us to be really enthusiastic about him emotionally, without even knowing who he actually is. In Romans 10:2 Paul is sad about people who are "zealous for God, but their zeal is not based on knowledge." Zeal means passion, and it's a great thing, but it has to be based on something real! I can feel like I really love my friend, but if I never make the time to talk with her, listening carefully to her story and getting to know who she really is, I'm not actually honoring her or loving her in any meaningful way. I'm essentially just guessing who she is, or making up who I want her to be, and loving the version of her in my imagination. We don't have to guess who God is, and we don't have the right to make up who we think he should be. He gave us the Bible because he wants us to know the truth about who he is. We honor and love him with our minds, when we're constantly seeking to grow in our understanding of who he actually is.

How do we do it?

This doesn't necessarily mean you need to read ten chapters of the Bible every day, or piles of Christian books, or listen to a sermon at night before bed. Sometimes we can easily get caught up thinking that putting more information *about* God into our heads is the same thing as knowing him more deeply. The Bible and books and sermons are fantastic, but what good is all that knowledge if we never really slow down and take the time to think it through and let it change us? Bible teacher Beth Moore says:

> "There is plenty of amazement in our church culture: churches that are amazing, events that are amazing. Books. Blogs. Tools. Software. Downloads. Bible studies. Preachers. Teachers. Worship leaders. We have more than enough amazement. Where change will come, however, is not in the amazement but in thinking it through. Meditating on it. Letting it sink in. Pondering what God has done. What God has made known. What God has brought to pass. We move on to the next thing too fast. You can't hear a still small voice, a gentle whisper when you are moving 100 miles per hour. Counter to your surrounding culture and maybe as the only person you know doing it, take the time to stop, push pause, and think about what God has said."[1]

She's saying that if we want to grow closer to God, we have to be disciplined enough to value quality over quantity. We need to sit with God in a quiet place away from distractions, slowly and prayerfully studying his Word, and listening to the Holy Spirit's gentle whisperings. We need to control the impulse to hurry, and learn to patiently contemplate instead. We need to reflect. We aren't learning about God so we can pass a test, we're learning about God so we can love him and worship him more.

---

1. Moore, "The Captivated Mind", 57.

Studying the Bible

There are lots of great ways to do your daily Bible study. Here are a few ideas:

- You can slowly work your way through a whole book of the Bible, studying one chapter or shorter passage each day. If reading lots isn't your thing, you can also listen to audio versions of the Bible. Don't avoid a book of the Bible just because it seems hard or irrelevant! God's given me wonderful glimpses of his glory in books of the Bible that I was honestly kind of dreading reading.

- Keep a journal, to record your prayers and reflections about what God is teaching you. This is one of my absolute favourite things to do. My mum inspired me to do this, because growing up I saw how she was reminded of all the ways God had faithfully answered her prayers. My journal is a record of my personal journey with God — all the ups and downs — and I absolutely love reading back over it and reflecting on how near God has been to me through even the hardest times in my life. It's so encouraging.

- Reading the Bible in community with others is also really important. Attend a Bible study group, or meet up with a friend once a week to study God's Word together. Regularly sharing your spiritual journey with others is a really important way to encourage one another, learn together, and hold each other accountable. It can be particularly useful if you're a verbal processor and need to talk things through out loud. Being mentored by a more mature Christian from your church is also a helpful way to wrestle with some of the harder questions or doubts you might have. Spiritual growth happens best when we're doing it in an honest, trusting community with other Christians.

God wants to show himself to you

Perhaps the idea of learning about God by studying the Bible stresses you out because you've struggled academically and don't think you're very smart. Maybe you find reading hard and you worry that you'll never understand enough. Memorize Matthew 11:25 and take heart! Jesus says, "I praise you, Father, Lord of heaven and earth, because you have hidden these things from the wise and learned, and revealed them to little children."

The Greatest Commandment — Part 3

God wants you to get to know him. He promises that if you seek him, you *will* find him. He's powerful enough to teach anyone's brain to understand anything. And he can also hide knowledge and wisdom from people if he wants, no matter how clever they are. You don't need to be super smart to love God. Pray that God will help you know him better today, with the particular brain he gave you. And be encouraged that there is not a single human being on earth who fully understands God: he's simply too big for our limited human minds! Thankfully for all of us, we aren't saved by how much we know about God or getting it perfectly right all the time.

Reflect and respond

1. Are you naturally someone whose relationship with God is more emotional, or more intellectual? How can you make sure you love God with both your heart and mind?
2. What stands out to you most from today's devotions, and why?

Open your Bible to Psalm 25.
Pray slowly through the first 11 verses, asking God to teach you his paths, to guide you in his truth, and to instruct you in his ways.

Meditation verse for the day:

Show me your ways, Lord, teach me your paths.
Guide me in your truth and teach me, for you are God my Savior,
and my hope is in you all day long.
(Psalm 25:4–5)

Day 49

The Greatest Commandment — Part 4

(Read Matthew 22:34–40)

The battle for your mind

Today we'll finish off discussing what it looks like to love God with all your mind. 2 Corinthians 10:5 tells us to "take captive every thought to make it obedient to Christ." This language of taking captives means to conquer our thoughts, to bring them forcefully under God's control. It sounds like the kind of language used in a war, because there actually *is* a spiritual battle happening for our minds. Our minds don't naturally trust God. We get easily confused and manipulated and tricked. We think wrongly. We lie to ourselves. We believe things that aren't true.

The way we fight the battle for our minds has two parts. Romans 12:2 tells us the first part: "Be transformed by the renewing of your mind." Our minds need to be made completely new from the inside out. That is work only the Holy Spirit can do. So pray every single day for your mind to be renewed! Continually ask for God to guard your thoughts, to purify the way you think, and to restore your mind to the way he created it to be. Humbly acknowledge that you can't do it alone, and you desperately need his power working inside you.

The second way we fight for our minds is our own responsibility. It's explained in Philippians 4:8: "Whatever is true, whatever is noble, whatever is right, whatever is pure, whatever is lovely, whatever is admirable — if anything is excellent or praiseworthy — think about such things." We have to make sure we're filling up our minds with things that are good. We have to focus on these things, concentrate on them, and saturate our thinking in them. We have to stop feeding our minds rubbish!

What are you feeding your mind?

Think back over the past few days. What sorts of music and TV shows have you filled up your brain with? What have you talked about with your friends? What have you looked at online? What have you day-dreamed about? As God's precious children and disciples of Jesus, what we put into our mind matters. In the same way that we have to take care of our bodies with nutritious food, we also have to take care of our minds with healthy content.

I've known suicidal teenagers who fill their heads with songs about death 24/7. I've heard of young kids who spend their free time watching internet porn, developing dangerous and degrading ideas of what sex is all about. I know depressed and angry young people who spend hours every day playing video games where the whole aim is to commit violent crimes. Many teenage girls have told me about their self-esteem issues or eating disorders, and then admit they spend most of their time looking at photos of celebrities on social media. Do we really need dozens of violent crime shows on TV? How about reality shows that are mostly people backstabbing one another and having drunken fights? Next time you listen to the radio, try to find a popular song that doesn't include unhealthy romantic relationships, or violence against women, or lyrics about getting wasted. It's almost impossible to do.

Neuroscientists tell us about an incredible thing called brain plasticity, where the connections in our brains grow and change in amazing ways. Brain plasticity means that the more we do a certain action or think in a certain way, the easier it becomes for us to do it again. If we do something over and over, our brain literally grows stronger and better and faster at doing that particular thing! That's why when we practice something lots, we gradually improve at it. We have to be particularly careful though, because it works both ways. If we practice thinking negatively, it will become easier and easier for us to think negatively as a habit. If we practice finding violence and drama exciting, we'll eventually start to find peace and kindness boring. If we practice criticizing every tiny imperfection we see on our bodies, we'll become experts at only seeing our flaws. You can see why it's so important for us to constantly guard our minds and pray for the Holy Spirit to renew our thinking.

There are lots of ways to practice focusing your mind on pure, noble, good things. Playing Christian music in the background of daily life can help us fix our eyes on who God is. We can read positive books and watch uplifting movies and listen to inspiring podcasts. We can explore nature and science and marvel at how amazingly artistic and thoughtful God is. We can put time into developing our own creative talents, making the world around us a more beautiful, flourishing place. There are so many wonders God has hidden in the incredible world around us! Let's invest our time into discovering and celebrating them, instead of spending hours scrolling mindlessly on our phones, filling our minds with shallow entertainment and then wondering why we're all getting more and more depressed and anxious.

Remembering and forgetting

All through the Bible, but particularly in the Old Testament, there's a cycle of God's people remembering and forgetting him. The Israelites repeatedly started to worship other gods every time they forgot the one true God. All the annual feasts and ceremonies that were built into their culture had a focus on celebrating and remembering God's goodness to them. We regularly see the authors of the psalms reminding themselves of what God did in the past, particularly when they're in trouble or feeling alone and afraid. David's response to tough times is to preach hard to his own heart and mind, telling himself to remember who God is.

If we forget who our God is, we won't want to spend time with him, we'll struggle to keep his commands, and other things take his place in the center of our hearts. The solution is to consciously focus our minds on remembering God. We have to keep reminding ourselves of the good news of the gospel. Keep repeating what we've learned about God's character and how much he loves us. Keep celebrating the stories of what he's done in our lives and our communities. Keep thanking him for his mercy and his grace. Keep telling others about his goodness to us. Keep writing down the glimpses we get of his blazing glory and his quiet beauty during our daily devotions. Keep memorizing Bible verses so that they're playing through our mind all day every day. Keep our mouths and hearts singing his praises. Remember, remember, remember.

Reflect and respond

1. *What thoughts has your mind told you are true, that go against what God tells you is true? i.e., you're worthless, there is no hope for the future, God doesn't care about you etc.*
2. *How will you deliberately fill your mind with good, noble, pure things this week?*
3. *What kinds of unhealthy content do you need to actively guard your mind against? How will you do that?*

Father God,
My mind is so saturated with the world's ideas and values that I find it hard to know what Truth really is.
Without your Word as an anchor I would be lost like a tiny boat being tossed on huge waves in the ocean.
Renew my mind. Help me to remember who you are and who I am in you.
Help me to focus my thoughts on good, noble, pure things.
I don't want to be like the world around me anymore, Lord.
I want to be like you.

In Jesus' name,
Amen

Meditation verse for the day:

Do not conform to the pattern of this world,
but be transformed by the renewing of your mind.
(Romans 12:2)

Day 50

The Second Greatest Commandment — Part 1

(READ MATTHEW 22:34–40)

The center of everything

Lots of non-Christian people admire Jesus. They even like these two great commands of his: love God and love other people. They wonder how the Jesus of the New Testament is such a caring guy, when God in the Old Testament just seems to be obsessed with giving huge lists of strict rules. But Jesus tells us something crucial in verse 40. He explains that *all* the other commands in the Bible are really just helping us to love God and to love other people. When he says "the Law and Prophets" he's referring to what we now call the Old Testament. So those laws God gave the ancient Israelites weren't him being harsh, they were all designed to teach the people how to love God better, and to love others well.

Jesus literally says all the Old Testament laws "hang on" these two commands. I imagine it like washing line with laundry hanging on it. Loving God and loving others are the washing line, holding up everything else. They're at the very foundation and center of every other command in the entire Bible. Pastor John Piper explains it like this:

> "I believe it would not be too much to say that all of creation, all of redemption, all of history, hang on these two great purposes – that

humans love God with all our heart, and that from the overflow of that love we love each other. Which means that love is the origin and the goal of the Law and Prophets. It is the beginning and the end of why God inspired the Bible."[1]

What a stunning idea of what life is all about! This one sentence from Jesus completely changes how we read the entire Bible, and how we think about our existence. Loving God and loving others is *everything*.

How can we love like this?

Jesus tells us here that loving God and loving the people around us comes before anything else in life. These two things should be what we spend most of our time and energy and passion and money on during the time we have on earth. They come before loving ourselves. They come before our own desires. They come before our own rights. They come before our own safety. They come before our own comfort. How does that make you feel? If it seems impossible to do (or even to *want* to do!), you're right; it is impossible without the transforming power of the Holy Spirit in our hearts.

There are so many verses about loving others in the Bible, but some of the most famous come from 1 John 4. You might already recognize some of these phrases:

- "Let us love one another, for love comes from God. Everyone who loves has been born of God and knows God." (verse 7)
- "God is love. Whoever lives in love lives in God, and God in them." (verse 16)
- "We love because he first loved us." (verse 19)

What's very clear from these verses is that our ability to love people comes from God living and working inside us. We won't be able to love others well if God the Spirit isn't renewing our hearts to make us more like Jesus. The kind of servant-hearted, self-sacrificial love Jesus is talking about goes completely against our nature. But when we start looking more and more like our Father, who is Love, we learn to speak like him, to act like him, to think like him, and to love like him.

---

1. Piper, "*Love Your Neighbour*".

Who do we love like this?

Jesus says we need to love our neighbors, but he isn't just talking about the people who live next door. He also isn't just talking about our friends and family, because in Matthew 5:46 he says that showing love to people who love us back is so easy even bad people do it. There's nothing counter-cultural or supernatural about it. So, who's our neighbor? Jesus is asked that exact question in Luke 10:29, and in response he tells the parable of the good Samaritan. This story explains that our neighbors include people who are our natural enemies, people who are very different to us in every way, people who it will cost us to care for, and people who we might normally avoid interacting with. Who might these people be in your own life? Who do you find it naturally uncomfortable to love?

An extraordinary number of times throughout the Bible, God's people are also specifically commanded to show *extra* love and care for poor people or people who are oppressed, particularly orphans, widows, and foreigners. In ancient Jewish culture these were people who had no power or rights, so they desperately needed others to care for them in order to survive. For God's people today, our list of people to show extra love to should include anyone who's left out or discriminated against in our communities: people who are bullied and lonely; people with mental health issues; people who are homeless; people who are refugees; people with intellectual or physical differences and disabilities; First Nations people; people struggling with addictions; elderly people; LGBTQ+ people; and people from ethnic or religious minorities.

The New Testament is also filled with dozens of commands for Christians to deeply love each other. In John 13:35 Jesus says the world will be able to tell we're his disciples if Christians all love each other the way that he loves us. It's meant to be what we're most well known for. We're told to be devoted to each other with our whole hearts, to serve one another in love, and to be united in passionate, humble love. This doesn't mean we'll all think the same way or always agree on everything, but it shows us that our faith in God should bring loving unity even to a group of people who might not have anything else in common.

So basically the Bible tells us we're called to love everyone. But God clearly puts a special emphasis on loving people who are different from us, people who are powerless in our communities, and people within God's own family. Because when our lives are defined by this kind of uncomfortable, costly love, the world will look at us and see that we're truly our Father's children. They'll look at us, and see him.

Reflect and respond

1. *What is something new or important that God is teaching you about himself through today's devotions?*
2. *Who do you struggle most to love in your life and why?*

God of love,
Thank you for your steadfast love.
Thank you that I am your treasured possession, your cherished bride.
Thank you that you have my name engraved forever on the palms of your hands.
Thank you that you loved me so much you sacrificed your Son Jesus to bring me back into your family.
Thank you that I am precious and honored in your sight.
I want your love to overflow out of me into the way I treat the people around me.
Help me love others as abundantly as you have loved me.
I want my life to radiate the love of Christ.

In Jesus' name,
Amen

Meditation verse for the day:

We love because he first loved us.
(1 John 4:19)

Day 51

The Second Greatest Commandment — Part 2

(Read Matthew 22:34–40)

Jesus tells us that the second most important thing to do with our time and energy and resources in life is to love others. But what exactly does he mean by love? Love in the Bible is much more than just a warm, fuzzy feeling. In 1 John 3:18 we're told not to just "love with words or speech but with actions and in truth." Love is something we *do*. We can't just talk about it, we have to live it with our actions. But the opposite is also true; love can't just be actions with no strong emotions. 1 Corinthians 13:3 says if we give everything we own to the poor but don't do it in love, it's completely worthless. To obey God and honor him, we're called to overflow with compassion and empathy and genuine care for others in helpful, life-giving ways.

Loving individuals

Some of the examples the Bible gives us of this love in action include:

- Being gentle and patient with each other (Ephesians 4:2)
- Being encouraging and building one another up (1 Thessalonians 5:11)
- Generously and joyfully sharing everything we have with whoever needs it (2 Corinthians 8:14)

- Feeding others, giving them clothes, and visiting them when they're sick or in prison (Matthew 25:35–36)
- Being kind and humble, being slow to anger, and not holding grudges (1 Corinthians 13:4–5)

This list challenges us to deny ourselves and put the needs and rights of others above our own. It's not enough to only give others our scraps or our spares. We can't only show love when it suits us, or when we have the energy, or when we can afford it. It's not about what fits neatly into our schedule or what feels natural to our personality. It's not about only loving people whose beliefs or lifestyles we approve of.

Like in the parable of the good Samaritan, God puts specific people in our path, and he calls us to love them in whatever way they need. This means we care for them even when it's inconvenient for us, and we show them kindness even when they don't deserve it. He's commanding us to love sacrificially. Why? Because that's how he loves us. Jesus' love for us on the cross was extravagantly and radically generous. He suffered for us. He gave up everything for us. He accepted the cost that should have been ours to pay. He is gentle and patient with us even when we reject and deny and crucify him. As Jesus' disciples, we're called to be like our Master. As God's children, we're called to be like our Father.

Building a loving society

God also gives lots of other commands to love that are about much more than being kind to individuals. He wants his people to build loving and just societies where every person is treated with dignity and respect. God commands us to make sure our communities look after the weak and powerless, and treat everyone fairly. Some examples of this kind of love in the Bible include:

- Defending oppressed people against injustice, and protecting the rights of vulnerable and powerless people (Isaiah 1:17, Psalm 82:3–4, and Zechariah 7:9–10)
- Treating immigrants equally and fairly under the law (Leviticus 24:22)
- Breaking down the unjust systems that oppress people (Isaiah 58:6)
- Not letting money unfairly influence the legal system so that wealthy people are treated better than poor people (Amos 5:12)

- Running businesses in a way that provides for needy people in the community, even though it cuts into profits (Leviticus 19:9–10)

We're commanded here to be advocates for others, which means we publicly support them. We act on their behalf to make sure they're always treated with mercy and justice regardless of their wealth or religion or family status or ethnicity or race or gender or age or sexuality or background or ability or visa status. We're called to go out of our way to publicly stand with the people who have no economic or social power, and make sure they're taken care of. Businesses are meant to operate for the good of society, and we're meant to work together to right wrongs that have happened in our communities.

These commands show us God's loving heart for all people, everywhere. They show us his love in action on a societal scale, bringing his upside-down kingdom values into our systems of government, our courts and prisons, our private businesses, and our public services like hospitals and schools.

Not one or the other, but both

It's likely that one type of neighborly love comes more naturally to you. Perhaps you find it easier to be patient and generous with individuals, but don't feel comfortable getting involved in biblical justice causes or public activism on behalf of the powerless and oppressed. It can be simpler to show daily kindness to the homeless person on your street, than to work with your local community leaders to stop people becoming homeless in the first place. Or maybe you love attending protests and signing petitions and standing up for the legal rights of disadvantaged groups, but find it too hard to actually build loving personal relationships with the complicated, messy, needy people around you. It can be easier to fight for laws that defend the lives of unborn babies, than to support a pregnant teenager or open up our homes and hearts to foster or adopt children who don't have families of their own.

But when Jesus tells us to love our neighbor, he isn't giving us a choice between the two different types of neighborly love. God commands us throughout the entire Bible to do *both*, all the time. We are to love our individual neighbors, and we're also called to contribute to building merciful, fair communities where everyone is treated with dignity and respect. So look around you and see who God has put around you to love. What are the needs that exist in your community? What skills and gifts can you invest in serving your neighborhood?

We know our personal relationships and societies will never be perfect on this side of heaven. Our hope is not in creating an ideal system of government that will change the world. Only Jesus can save people, not great laws or community programs or healthy relationships. But Christians are still called to bring the transforming power of the gospel into every area of life, both personal and communal. Why? Because when we do, we reflect the character of our Father.

We serve a God who identifies himself as the defender of widows and orphans, and who says he hears the cries of the poor and personally avenges the oppressed. To show the world who this God is, we should be known as people who are characterized by love. Christians should have a reputation as people who work tirelessly for restoration and renewal and redemption and reconciliation in every corner of our hurting world. Everything we do should point others to this God who carefully heals the broken-hearted and tenderly cares for the needy and is passionate about bringing justice to people no one else cares about.

Reflect and respond

1. *Look through the examples of neighborly love. Which of these do you find the hardest to do, and why?*
2. *Think about the individual people God has placed in your life. Who are two people that God might be calling you love well right now? What are some practical ways can you show them love by meeting their needs?*
3. *Think about the community that God has put you in right now. It might be your street, neighborhood, school, or workplace. What are two practical ways you can be an advocate for vulnerable and disadvantaged people in your community?*

Turn to Psalm 146 in your Bible.
Pray slowly through this psalm, meditating on the beauty of God's compassion, and his heart for merciful justice.

Meditation verse for the day:

And what does the Lord require of you?
To act justly and to love mercy
and to walk humbly with your God.
(Micah 6:8)

Day 52

Don't Be a Pharisee — Part 1

(READ MATTHEW 23:1–22)

IN THIS PASSAGE JESUS is once again speaking to the teachers of the Jewish religious law and the Pharisees. He uses some of his strongest language here, and it's clear he's *very* angry! It's easy to assume he's not also talking to us personally here, but please pray God would show you areas of your own life that are more like the Pharisees' than you'd like to admit.

Don't be a hypocrite

In verses 3–4, Jesus criticizes the religious leaders for not practicing what they preach. They teach other people a whole lot of stuff about God, but they don't actually honor God in their own hearts and lives! Many of us are hypocrites as well. We say one thing and do something totally different. Maybe we act a different way on Sundays at church than we do the rest of the week. We might passionately sing worship songs about following Jesus, but then live most of life as if he doesn't really matter. We might expect other people to forgive us when we mess up, but hold onto grudges against them when they hurt us.

Check your motivation

In verses 5–12, the next huge issue Jesus has with the religious leaders is that they're way too concerned with what other people think. They do all the good things religious Jewish people are meant to do, but they aren't doing any of it out of love for God! The phylacteries he mentions in verse 5 are small boxes devout Jewish men wear on their foreheads while they pray, and tassels are long strings that hang down from the corners of their prayer shawls. Jesus probably wore phylacteries and tassels himself, as a Jewish rabbi. Jesus isn't against these customs at all, but he has no patience for people who do them for the wrong reasons. They're meant to remind the person wearing them of God, but these religious leaders make their phylacteries bigger than normal and their tassels longer than anyone else's, so they look more religious than other people. They just want others to admire and respect them, and they want praise for how holy they are. They care too much about their reputation, and think they're better than everyone else. Their hearts aren't focused on God, only on themselves.

Jesus reminds us in verse 11 that greatness in the kingdom of God isn't about being publicly respected or being a popular leader or famous preacher. It's about being a servant. It's about faithfully serving God and the people around us in genuine love. That's the kind of worship God wants from us, and that's the kind of attitude that brings him joy and glory.

So think about it carefully: why are you a Christian? What motivates you to show kindness to the people around you? Why do you wear that big cross necklace or have that Bible verse tattoo? Why do you have all those notes written in your Bible? Why do you lift up your hands in worship? Why do pray the way you do? Is it all for others to see? So that you can feel good about yourself? Or is your deepest desire to know and love and honor God with everything you do?

Tradition vs. the Bible

In verses 16–22 Jesus turns his attention to the fact that the religious leaders add their own human traditions to what the Bible says. They've created extra rules and laws for holiness, and invented technicalities and loopholes for people to be able to get out of doing the right thing. The example Jesus gives here is that they offer people official ways to get out of keeping a promise by saying it all depends on exactly what they swore by. They're completely missing God's main point, which is that we should be honourable and keep our word.

Like the Pharisees, we all have a dangerous habit of picking and choosing the parts of God's Word we prefer, or of adding extra rules to live by that help us feel comfortable. It's why we need to read the Bible every day for ourselves, so we can learn to recognize God's holy intentions and purposes behind his commands, and make sure we're obeying his heart. Just because something is a tradition doesn't mean it's wrong or bad, but we have to know the difference between a human tradition and God's commands. Our ultimate allegiance should only ever be to God's Word.

One way we do this is by using our cultural traditions as an excuse for unbiblical ways of living. All cultures are a beautiful part of God's diverse creation, but that doesn't mean every single part of every single culture is honoring to God. Human cultures are damaged by sin just like individuals are. There are some parts of every culture that are beautiful and good, and some parts of every culture that are evil and sinful. For example, some cultures prioritize material wealth and say that our value in life comes from how much we earn, which is completely against what the Bible says. Other cultures idolize working too hard to rest on the Sabbath, which ignores God's commands. Many cultures say that men are more valuable and important than women, which is completely unbiblical. In lots of places around the world people who have a different skin color or religion or language are treated like they're worth less than others, but God says every one of us is created in his image and is loved equally by him. As Christians, we have to check everything our culture tells us against what the Bible says, testing whether it's good and right. We have to put God's kingdom's culture before our human traditions.

The other extreme is when people add extra rules for righteousness to the Bible. We might get taught that to be saved, we're never allowed to drink alcohol, or we have to wear certain clothes to church. Those are not God's commands and do not come from the Bible — they're human traditions. They aren't going to save you one way or the other. God alone saves us by his grace, when we turn to him in repentance. There's nothing else we need to do.

Reflect and respond

1. *When do you struggle to practice what you preach? When do you hold others to a higher standard than you hold yourself?*
2. *What are some ways the values of God's kingdom are very different to the values of your culture?*

Merciful God,
I'm so much more like the Pharisees than I like to admit.
I'm a hypocrite.
I care too much about what others think of me.
I find it more comfortable to live by my own standards than by yours.
Please forgive me.
Thank you that your mercies are new every morning.
Today, please help me to be a little less like a Pharisee and a little more like Jesus.

In Jesus' name,
Amen

Meditation verse for the day:

The Lord says: "These people come near to me with their mouth
and honor me with their lips, but their hearts are far from me.
Their worship of me is based on merely human rules
they have been taught."
(Isaiah 29:13)

Day 53

Don't Be a Pharisee — Part 2

(Read Matthew 23:23–39)

Lacking justice and mercy and faithfulness

Jesus is still talking angrily to the same group of religious leaders as yesterday. Now he accuses them of following all the Bible's laws but completely missing the main point. Jesus' example about tithing in verse 23 shows how absurd their actions are. Tithing means to give 10 percent of everything we have to God. Instead of simply giving 10 percent of their pay to the temple, the religious leaders even tithe the tiny herbs from their gardens! That's not necessarily a bad thing, but once again they've missed God's whole point in giving that command in the first place.

Remember how Jesus told us in Matthew 22:40 that all the Old Testament laws existed to help the Israelites love God and love others better? He's saying here that the legalistic Pharisees are so focused on making sure they give exactly a tithe of every little thing they own, they forget all about this overarching purpose behind God's commands: loving God faithfully and showing each other justice and mercy.

We can laugh at the ridiculous picture of the Pharisees going around their gardens, smugly counting each and every individual mint leaf, but we all need to take a hard look at our own lives to make sure we don't do the same thing. We all find it easier to see Christianity as a checklist of actions we can tick off, feeling proud at the end of the day because we've done all the good things and avoided most of the bad things.

Jesus is challenging all of us here to see that God calls us to much more than just morally good behaviors. He says in verse 23 that the most important parts of all God's commands are "justice, mercy, and faithfulness." He wants to know, do we faithfully love God with our whole heart and soul and mind? And are we also showing love to the people around us? Do we have compassion for the lonely and the outcasts? Do we stand up for people who are getting left out? Are we welcoming towards people who have very different beliefs or lifestyles from us? Do we show forgiveness and mercy to people who have hurt us? Are we known for defending the rights of people who aren't able to speak up for themselves?

It's what's on the inside that counts

Then in verses 25–32, Jesus calls the religious leaders hypocrites again, three times in a row! He is furious with them for focusing so much on outward appearances and completely ignoring what's going on inside their hearts. They care so much about looking good to the people around them, that they never get around to dealing with the hidden sin deep inside them. Who wants to drink out of a cup that's clean on the outside but is completely filthy on the inside? It's useless to anyone. And what good is it to decorate a tomb beautifully when it's filled with rotten, stinking bones?

God is not honored at all by how righteous we look on the outside. We can do all the right things and look like great Christians to everyone else, but he sees what's really on the inside. He isn't expecting us to be perfect, because he knows we can't be. He's actually asking us to *stop pretending* we're perfect. When we hide our sin away and pretend it's not there, we're just lying to ourselves and others. As Christians, we should be the world's greatest experts at admitting we're wrong and humbly asking for forgiveness — from God and from the people around us. If you haven't repented for anything recently, ask the Holy Spirit to show you an area of sin in your heart that you need to focus on. The purpose of this is not to make you feel bad: it's to set you free and help you grow to be more like Jesus!

Jesus' anger

It's worth backing up for a moment and reflecting on how angry Jesus is here. In this chapter, he pronounces "Woe to you!" on the religious leaders seven times. 'Woe' is a word used throughout the Bible as a strong warning of God's coming judgment. He uses really emotional and emphatic language here, calling them children of hell, blind fools, snakes and vipers, and murderers! Make no mistake: *Jesus is absolutely livid*. He's angry because these leaders are abusing their authority and getting in the way of other people being saved. He's angry because vulnerable people are being led astray by the people they should be able to trust most. He's angry because the leaders of God's chosen people have the same values as the world, not the servant-hearted values of God. He's angry because these leaders aren't characterized by the two things closest to God's own heart: faithful love for God and mercy and justice towards each other. He's angry because God isn't getting the honor he deserves.

This passage reminds us that some anger is righteous. There are some things in life that it's right to get really angry about, like honouring God faithfully and serving others well. There are times when it's appropriate to use forceful language in speaking the truth. There are times when love in action doesn't sound mild and gentle and tender. What kind of things make you angry? How can you make sure your anger is righteous?

Jesus is our mother hen

Jesus' wrath is powerful but brief. If we look back at Matthew's Gospel as a whole, Jesus isn't mainly an angry person. He doesn't use up most of his breath protesting loudly for truth, publicly calling people out for their sins. His fierce anger is the exception to how he relates to others, not the rule. He's mainly gentle and loving. He's mainly welcoming and tender. He's mainly deavasted by the effects of sin.

Verse 37 is incredibly powerful and emotional – read it again. And again. Jesus has gone from being extremely angry at the Pharisees and teachers of the law, to suddenly being completely heartbroken. He's deeply grieving over Jerusalem's people, who he knows are going to kill him in just a few days. *Jerusalem, Jerusalem!* Hear the anguish in his voice. He doesn't hate them for rejecting him, he feels deep sadness for them.

In verse 37 Jesus gives us a beautiful visual image of himself as a mother hen, spreading her wings to protect her vulnerable chicks from harm. He mourns that people turn down his free offer of salvation. He grieves that people won't let him provide them with safety and security. This is the reason why he cried as he rode into Jerusalem on the donkey just a few days before. His heart breaks with tender love for the people who reject him. He longs for us all to just let him love us.

The world tells us that Christianity takes away our rights and our freedoms, and limits the fun we'll have in life. This is what Jesus tells us being a Christian means: taking shelter under the powerful wings of our loving mother hen, who promises to give us safety and rest like we've never experienced before. He invites us to come in out of the storm and finally find abundant peace with the one who loves us the most.

Reflect and respond

1. What needs to change in your life to make sure that faith, mercy and justice are at the very center of who you are and how you live?
2. We live in a world that thrives on outrage, where people love to tear each other down in the name of 'truth'. How can you be characterized by loving kindness, instead of by anger and bitterness?
3. Reflect on the metaphor of Jesus as a caring mother hen in verse 37. How does this picture lead you to worship God?

Lord,
I don't want to be righteous on the outside and filthy on the inside.
I don't want to do good things but miss the things that matter most to God.
I know that only you can fix the mess I am on the inside.
Clean me, Lord.
Thank you for how tenderly you love your children.
You are a good, good Father.

In Jesus' name,
Amen

Meditation verse for the day:

My sacrifice, O God, is a broken spirit;
a broken and contrite heart you, God, will not despise.
(Psalm 51:17)

Day 54

Keep Watch

(Read Matthew Chapter 24)

This is a pretty long, detailed passage, and it's not a very uplifting topic. Jesus is telling his disciples that lots of terrible things are going to happen before Judgment Day finally comes. It's really easy to get distracted trying to figure out exactly which historical wars and famines and earthquakes Jesus might have been referring to, to work out when he's going to return. We could spend our lives trying to read all the clues in the Bible and figure it out, but we'd be wasting our time. Jesus makes it really clear that only God knows when Judgement Day will happen, and that it'll come when no one expects it.

Preparing for the end of the world

Jesus' main point in this passage is extremely important for us to understand. In verses 42–51 he says that because we don't know when the end of the world will be, we need to be ready for it to happen at any time. That's our responsibility. We never know when the end might come. You might have already lived the majority of your time on earth. So what does it look like to be ready for Judgment Day? As we've seen over and over through the book of Matthew, God is most interested in where your heart is at. If you've humbly repented for trying to be the lord of your own life and are trusting in Jesus to save you, you're ready for Judgement Day! Your huge debt has been completely paid and wiped away forever, and you'll be welcomed into heaven's feast dressed in Jesus' own perfect wedding clothes.

Don't relax too soon though. Just because we know we've been adopted into God's family doesn't mean we should just cruise through the rest of life on autopilot. We're in the middle of a fierce spiritual battle. The devil will be trying anything he can to distract us with the delights and disappointments of the world, and we don't want to become the people in verse 12 whose love for God slowly fades away over time. We need to keep fighting for Jesus to be our heart's treasure every single day. We need to keep surrendering our lives to God's lordship. We need to keep humbly seeking to put God first in our hearts and souls and minds, asking the Holy Spirit to teach us and change us. We have to constantly reflect on if we're actually trusting in Jesus alone for salvation, not in our good works like the Pharisees. Remember, the Pharisees thought they were definitely going to heaven, but Jesus makes it clear that they weren't! That is a clear warning for us all to stay spiritually alert every day of our lives.

Don't waste your life

Part of being ready for the end of the world also involves living intentionally. Verse 45 describes the "faithful and wise servant" who diligently and consistently does what the master has asked while he's away. What has God asked you to do with the time he's given you? Here's a hint: it probably revolves in some way around loving God and loving other people. What unique gifts and skills and passions has God given you, that you can use to honor him in your one life? How can you love God and love your neighbors faithfully with everything you've been given? It looks different for each of us. Pastor John Piper says it like this in his powerful book *Don't Waste Your Life*: "But whatever you do, find the God-centered, Christ-exalting, Bible-saturated passion of your life, and find your way to say it and live it and die for it. And you will make a difference that lasts. You will not waste your life."[1]

So what does it look like to invest our days on earth into eternity? When you stand before God's throne and he asks what you've spent the days and weeks and months and years of your life doing, what will be your answer? It would be devastating to have nothing to show the Lord of all

---

1. Piper, *Don't Waste Your Life*, 47.

Keep Watch

Creation except a high video-game score, or a bunch of likes on social media, or a bank account full of money.

The main way you might think of honoring God is to share the good news of Jesus. That's a great way to spend your life, and it's definitely something Jesus tells all Christians to do. We should all long to bring others to heaven along with us. He's placed you exactly where you are today for a reason. Look around you. Who can you show God's love to, right where you are? Who needs some gentle encouragement? Who needs to hear the amazing news that Jesus delights in them? Be courageous: the Holy Spirit lives in you! Don't underestimate his power working in and through you to change the lives of the people around you.

God doesn't tell us a whole lot of specifics about what eternity in heaven will be like, but we do know it will be a beautiful garden-city brimming with all the highlights of human creativity from throughout history. Revelation 21:26 tells us that "the glory and honor of the nations" will be there with us in heaven. Isaiah 60 tells us the best things from all human cultures will be in heaven to beautify it, as an adornment to make it all even more glorious. Imagine all the absolute best parts of every single society throughout human history, everything beautiful that has ever been created and cultivated by human beings, purified somehow so it's completely perfect and holy. Art and music and sports and cultural dances. Pyramids and skyscrapers and jewellery and Lamborghinis. Poems written by children. Secret family recipes from kitchens all over the globe. All of the good things, without any of the bad. Every time you create and build and act for God's glory, you could be leaving ripples in eternity. Every time you seek to worship God through your daily loving and serving and working, you could be adding gorgeous decorations to heaven, to delight God and his children forever. And yet even all of the wonders of the earth will be nothing more than decorations around the edges of heaven compared with the glory of being in God's presence. Doesn't it make your heart sing?

Reflect and respond

1. *If Judgement Day comes today, are you ready? Why, or why not?*
2. *How does today's devotions challenge you?*
3. *How does today's devotions encourage you?*

Father in heaven,
Hallowed be your name.
You are so worthy of the highest praise!
Your kingdom come, your will be done on earth as it is in heaven.
Reign over us, Lord of lords and King of kings.
Give me today my daily bread.
I trust that you know what I need better than I do.
Forgive me my debts as I have also forgiven my debtors.
I repent for my rebellion against you. Forgive me.
Please soften my heart so I can forgive others.
Lead me not into temptation, but deliver me from evil.
Guard my heart and my life from the traps and distractions of the devil.
Help me stand firm in faithfulness and obedience.
I want my life to honor you. I want to build for eternity.
I love you.

In Jesus' name,
Amen.

Meditation verse for the day:

So you also must be ready, because the Son of Man will come at an hour when you do not expect him.
(Matthew 24:44)

Day 55

Parables about Being Prepared

(Read Matthew 25:1–30)

Parable of the ten virgins

This chapter starts with the parable of the ten virgins, which has the same main message as yesterday's passage. The ten young virgins are bridesmaids who have been given the important job of meeting the bridegroom outside with lamps as he arrives at his wedding. He takes longer to arrive than expected, and because some of the women are not organized enough, their lamps run out of oil so their flames go out. They run off to find some more fuel for their lamps, but while they're gone the groom arrives and the wedding banquet begins without them. Once again, Jesus is warning us to stay spiritually alert. We never know when Jesus our bridegroom is going to come back, and we absolutely do not want to miss the wedding feast.

The Parable of the Bags of Gold

Jesus' parable in verse 14 is on the same theme, but now he puts more emphasis on what we do with our time on earth. A master is going away for a while, so he splits up his wealth between his servants so they can look after it for him. In some Bible translations it says he gives out bags of gold, and in others it calls them talents. A talent was a huge sum of money, probably worth around half a million dollars. Whichever translation you read, three things are very clear from the start:

1. Everything the servants have was given to them as a gift and a responsibility, out of the generosity of the master.
2. The servants didn't all get given equal amounts.
3. Every servant received a gift of great value.

Equal in worth but not in talents

The bags of gold in this parable are a metaphor for the skills and abilities we've all been given by God. Every single one of us was created in God's image and we're all equally important and valuable to him. However, in his wisdom he's chosen not to give us all the same gifts in life. Some of us are really good at using our brains to think analytically. Some of us are creative and artistic. Some of us are athletic. Some of us are great at relating to people. Some people are leaders, and others work best behind the scenes supporting those who lead.

This doesn't mean God is unfair. He created us, and the gifts all belong to him in the first place. Doesn't he have the right to share them however he thinks is best? 1 Corinthians 12:12–27 gives us a wonderful picture of what this means in the world-wide church. Paul describes us as different parts making up the body of Christ together; some of us are feet, some are eyes, some are ears. The body just wouldn't work if we were all heads! We each have a different role to play, but every role has dignity and value. And we all need each other and support one another, working together in unity so that the whole body flourishes. Verse 18 explains that "God has placed the parts in the body, every one of them, just as he wanted them to be."

God has a wonderful plan for the salvation of his chosen people throughout history. He could easily do it all by himself, but instead he invites us to participate and contribute! How incredible is that? He gives us all unique talents so we can each play a different role in his story. He's deliberately put you exactly where you are, with the unique skills that you have, for a particular reason. As Tim Keller says, "There are some needs only you can see. There are some hands only you can hold. There are some people only you can reach."[1] What a privilege to get to partner with God

---

1. Keller, Twitter Post, August 14, 2021

in his amazing plan to bring people to know him, and to help restore and redeem all the parts of his beautiful creation.

We see from this parable that glorifying God with our skills and talents isn't just a privilege, it's also a responsibility. As the Giver, God has every right to expect us not to waste our gifts. Look at how the master reacts to the servants who have carefully and wisely invested their bags of gold in verses 21 and 23. He says, "Well done, good and faithful servant!" and then he promises them even more gifts and honor and joy in the future. But as for the servant who did nothing with his bag of gold, the master calls him wicked and lazy and kicks him out of his household into the darkness. Wasting your talents is offensive to God, who gave them to you for a reason. We've all been generously given specific gifts, and we're personally responsible for doing something with them that honors our loving Father.

Which bag of gold did you get?

Maybe you look around and feel like the only person who doesn't have any skills that make you special. Maybe you struggle with feeling inadequate. Perhaps you're jealous or bitter at God, like the third servant, because you feel like he didn't give you any worthwhile talents. Be encouraged that God doesn't leave any of us without gifts. Like the servants in this parable, every single one of us has been given incredibly valuable, important talents. They're just all different. There's a very wise saying: "Comparison is the thief of joy". Going through life constantly comparing ourselves to others will only lead to discontent and disappointment. When we envy other's gifts or feel insecure or jealous because we're not as talented as they are, we're actually looking down on the unique and special abilities that God's given us. We're telling him we don't like his gifts. Instead, pray God will help you see and appreciate the particular talents he's given you, and help you know how to use them in life-giving and creative ways!

Or perhaps you're more like the servant who got five huge bags of gold. Do you just seem to succeed at everything you do? Do you excel in lots of different areas? This parable reminds us that none of us can boast about the skills we have, or take credit for them ourselves, because they're a generous gift from God. We didn't do anything to deserve them or earn them. We also shouldn't look down on people who don't have the natural abilities we have, because they are just as precious to God as we are. Their role in the body of Christ is just as important to him. And we should never forget the warning in Luke 12:48: "From everyone who has been given much, much will be demanded; and from the one who has been entrusted with much, much more will be asked." This means the more gifts we've been given in life, the more Jesus will hold us accountable for using them well.

Reflect and respond

1. What is something from today's devotions that you can gratefully praise God for?
2. How can you guard your heart against feeling jealous over the gifts God has given someone else?

Most High God,
The earth is yours, and everything in it.
The world and all its people belong to you.
You own the cattle on a thousand hills, and all the animals of the forest.
Every good and perfect gift comes from you.
Everything around me and in me was created by you and through you, and exists for you.
May I use the talents you've so generously given me to bring honor to your name.
Yours is the glory forever and ever.

In Jesus' name,
Amen

Meditation verse for the day:

Well done, good and faithful servant!
You have been faithful with a few things;
I will put you in charge of many things.
Come and share your master's happiness!
(Matthew 25:23)

Day 56

The Sheep and the Goats

(READ MATTHEW 25:31–46)

IN THIS PASSAGE JESUS is still talking about Judgment Day, when all people will stand before him to be judged for all eternity. This is very, very serious stuff. He describes separating all humans into two groups, the sheep and the goats. The sheep are the children of God, and in verse 34 he promises we'll inherit something stunning from our loving Father: "the Kingdom prepared for you since the creation of the world." Wow! God's been working on heaven specifically with us in mind since time began! It's actually impossible to wrap our minds around what that will be like!

The people represented by goats, though, will spend the rest of eternity in fire, together with the devil and all his evil spirits. This may not mean literal fire, but even if it's just a metaphor it's clear there's absolutely nothing good about it. Some people joke that hell will be more fun than heaven, but the Bible tells us it'll actually be the complete absence of God's loving presence and anything that flows from his character: absolutely no love, no joy, no goodness, no wisdom, no beauty, no kindness, nothing honorable or noble or right . . . for all eternity. That sounds devastatingly hopeless.

Mercy and love

It's fascinating to hear Jesus describe the difference between the sheep and the goats in verses 35–40. We would expect Jesus to separate us based on whether we trust him as our Lord and Savior, but instead he focuses on the fruit of faith in our lives. The sheep acted with mercy and compassion and love towards others, but the goats didn't. He wants to see evidence that our faith is real. If we're truly his disciples, the way we treat others should prove it. The Apostle Paul puts it this way in Galatians 5:6: "The only thing that counts is faith expressing itself through love." Real faith will always show up as love for others. Anyone can think they trust in Jesus, but if our faith is alive then it'll be obvious by how we supernaturally love the people around us.

Once again, Jesus doesn't let us off the hook by only holding us responsible for loving our friends. He says his true disciples will show compassion for the people the rest of society doesn't consider worth caring for. People who are too poor to have access to food and water. Foreigners and immigrants. Sick people. Criminals in prison. These are people who might be hard to love. These are people who might not deserve to be helped. They might be a huge burden on us emotionally or financially. None of that matters to Jesus. He explains that every time we lovingly serve these people, it's as if we're doing it for him personally.

As we've seen, this focus on caring for needy people is a consistent theme throughout Jesus' life and the entire Bible. Jesus' brother James emphasized showing practical love to the poor, and wrote "religion that God our Father accepts as pure and faultless is this: to look after orphans and widows in their distress" (James 1:27). There's a lot of talk about the appropriate role of 'social justice' in the church, and many Christians divide down political and ideological lines. Don't let politicians or even Christian leaders tell you what to think on this subject. Listen to Jesus' own words. *This* is what Jesus says matters to him. *This* is how he'll know who his true disciples are.

A tree is recognized by its fruit

A common way we can completely miss the heart of God, is to treat people like spiritual projects. We might happily serve their needs, but only as a way of getting them to listen to us tell them about God. We might accept the cost of loving them, but only because we hope eventually they'll become Christians as a result. We approach loving them as a spiritual strategy, like an investment we're expecting to pay off. This isn't genuine love, and it isn't treating that person with dignity and respect. It's loving with strings attached, caring with an ulterior motive. Jesus doesn't separate the sheep and the goats based on how many people we share the gospel with. He doesn't separate the sheep and the goats based on how many people we convert to Christianity. He simply asks how we care for the people our society doesn't value.

Does your heart break for the things that God's heart breaks for? When you look at your lifestyle, is it characterized by care for needy, hurting people? Do you regularly see the people on the margins of your world and go out of your way to show them love? Do you look at the people your community pushes to the side, and recognize that they're made in the image of Almighty God? Are you willing to sacrifice your own comfort and resources for someone who might not even deserve or appreciate your help? Jesus tells us that trees are recognized by their fruit. What does the fruit in your life show about your tree?

We're saved by God's gift of grace, not by our actions

We have to be very careful with passages like this, not to take them out of context. Jesus is not saying that all you have to do for salvation is show mercy to poor people. There are plenty of very kind people out there who don't love God at all, but they care selflessly for people on the edges of society. He's also not saying that if our levels of justice and mercy are good enough we'll earn ourselves a spot in heaven. That wouldn't be consistent with what is said in dozens of other parts of the Bible, so it's clearly not what he means here. The Bible says over and over that we're saved *only* by God's free gift of grace, not by anything that we do. It's not loving others that saves us. In fact, it's possible to even become self-righteous about how much we care for hurting people! We can easily become just as prideful as the Pharisees, if we start to trust in how loving we are for salvation.

Jesus is actually highlighting here that one of the clearest signs we have really been adopted into God's family, is that we've started to become like our new Father. We've grown to love the things that he loves, and to care about the things that he cares about. There's a strong family resemblance that the Holy Spirit brings about in our personality and our character and our actions over time. Loving others doesn't save us; loving others is evidence we've already been saved. Our God has a burning passion for protecting and saving vulnerable, hurting people. Others should be able to look at the way we selflessly love and serve the most powerless people in our communities, and know exactly who our Father is.

Reflect and respond

1. What do we learn about God's heart from today's devotions?
2. What fruit is growing in your life? Who are you becoming?

Loving Father,
You are a Father to the fatherless, and a defender of widows.
You give lonely people families, and you lead prisoners out of their chains with singing.
You provide abundant rains to those wandering in the dry desert, and you refresh the weary.
You carry my burdens for me.
You loved me when I was your enemy.
I want to be like you.
I want to love generously, abundantly, and deeply.
I want to love others even when they're unlovable.
Put your love in my heart for the hurting people around me.
Open my eyes to see them as you see them.

In Jesus' name,
Amen

Meditation verse for the day:

Religion that God our Father accepts as pure and faultless is this:
to look after orphans and widows in their distress
and to keep oneself from being polluted by the world.
(James 1:27)

Day 57

The Perfume and the Plot

(READ MATTHEW 26:1–16)

VERSE 1 SHOWS THAT Jesus knows he's very close to dying a horrible death. In the meantime, he's the guest of honor at a friend's dinner party, in the small village of Bethany just outside Jerusalem. During the meal, a woman poured very expensive perfume over him. We know from the parallel version of this story in John 12 that the woman was Mary, one of Jesus' close friends and the sister of Martha and Lazarus. That version of the story also tells us that the perfume was worth about a year's salary!

Jesus is her treasure

Through this beautiful and costly action, Mary's putting her love for Jesus on display for everyone to see. Jesus had recently raised her beloved brother Lazarus from the dead (see John 11 for the full story), and she's probably still feeling overwhelmed with gratitude. She's seen Jesus' power and glory in action up close, and she's in awe of him. She deliberately chooses her most precious possession to sacrifice publicly for Jesus, to show him how much she adores him. She wants him to know she sees his true worth. She wants to show the world that he means more to her than anything else, and that he's worth any sacrifice to her.

Can you see the difference between Mary and the Pharisees? The Pharisees behave right and look super holy, but it's ultimately all about them. They like feeling good about themselves and being respected by the people around them. Unlike them, all Mary's devotion and attention are completely centered on Jesus. She's not just doing things out of a sense of duty. Her emotions are fully engaged, and she's joyful and thankful that Jesus is her friend. She delights in him. She's wants to give him a gift that's worthy of who he is. She wants to make the most of every moment she gets with him. She doesn't even stop to wonder if others will ridicule her.

When you read this story, what's your immediate reaction to Mary's sacrifice? Do you think her actions were over the top? Does it seem like a bit of a waste? Or do you see the beauty in what she did? Jesus' response in verses 10–13 shows that he's pleased by Mary's display of love for him. He doesn't tell her off for using up all her expensive perfume in a single moment. He interprets what she did as a beautiful and appropriate act of worship, and he honors her for it. It reminds me of the elders around God's throne in Revelation 4, laying their crowns before him in worship. When the Holy Spirit opens our eyes to see Jesus' true worth, we won't want to give him any less than the very best we have. We know he's worthy of our crowns, which means all our achievements and skills and glory and treasures. We long to lay them all at his feet as an offering of adoration.

But some of the disciples aren't happy. In verse 8 we see that all they can think about is the amount of money Mary just poured out onto the floor, and they feel like it was a complete waste. To be fair, their argument sounds pretty solid. Giving a whole lot of money to poor people is the exact kind of thing Jesus would normally want his followers to do! They judge Mary loudly, maybe trying to shame her in front of all the other guests. John 12's version of this story tells us that Judas is particularly upset about Mary's actions, but not because he cares for poor people. He wants the money from the sale of Mary's perfume in the disciples' money bag, because he's the one in charge of carrying it around. In fact, we learn that he regularly steals money from the group's money bag! So when he sees that expensive perfume dripping down off Jesus onto the floor, all he can think about are the huge piles of money that had almost been his.

What we worship controls us

All human beings worship something. We were created by God to find our true selves in worshipping him, but we would rather choose to worship other things. Some of us worship money, others worship power. We might worship relationships, or our achievements. Many of us worship ourselves:

our feelings or our identities. We worship our independence. The thing we worship is the idol that has stolen our heart away from belonging to God alone. The thing we worship is what we think we need most to feel secure and happy. This means the thing we worship drives our daily decisions and our emotions. It controls us.

For example, someone who worships the approval of others will do anything to make sure people like them. They'll compromise their values, stay in unhealthy relationships for far too long, or desperately avoid conflict, all to make sure people don't stop giving them the approval they feel like they need. They're controlled by their desire to be liked.

Judas worships money. It's no coincidence that immediately after this controversial dinner party, Judas goes to the chief priests and offers to betray Jesus to them for thirty pieces of silver. Money is the treasure of his heart. He's feeling jealous and bitter about the small fortune Mary just poured over Jesus, and he's probably furious with Jesus for allowing it to happen. His greed is driving all of his choices, and he's willing to do whatever it takes to get more money, including betraying one of his closest friends.

Mary worships Jesus. Her love for Jesus led her to sacrifice her expensive perfume. Her wonder at his majesty and holiness and compassion controls the way she lives her life. It shapes the choices she makes and even the emotions she feels. Jesus is what our hearts were made to worship from the moment we were created, so he's the only one who will ever really satisfy us. He's the only one who will really bring us the lasting joy and meaning that we all crave. He's the only one who's worthy of any sacrifice we'll ever make for him.

Reflect and respond

1. What do you worship? To answer this, reflect on:
   - What gives you your deepest joy and confidence?
   - What do you depend on for comfort when life is hard?
   - What do you feel like you couldn't live without?
   - What is at the center of all your daydreams about the future?
2. How does what you worship control how you live your life? How does it control your decision-making, and how you think and feel and behave?

Turn in your Bible to Psalm 100. Pray through it slowly, worshipping the Lord in wonder, and reflecting on his supreme worthiness.

Meditation verse for the day:

They lay their crowns before the throne and say:
"You are worthy, our Lord and God,
to receive glory and honor and power,
for you created all things, and by your will
they were created and have their being."
(Revelation 4:10–11)

Day 58

The Last Supper and the Garden of Gethsemane

(Read Matthew 26:17–46)

It's Thursday night, the night before Jesus' crucifixion. He and his disciples are doing the same thing they do every year at this time: celebrating the Passover with a meal of lamb and flat bread. They eat remembering how God had rescued their ancestors from slavery in Egypt all those centuries ago. They sing traditional Passover songs together, probably from Psalms 113–118. In the parallel story in Luke 22, Jesus tells his disciples he's really been looking forward to this final meal together before he suffers. He knows what's about to happen to him, and what he wants most is to spend his last night in fellowship with his closest friends, celebrating the faithfulness and mercy of their Father together!

The Lord's Supper

There are never accidents with God, and the fact that Jesus' death happens on Passover weekend is definitely not a coincidence. In the very first Passover in Exodus 12, a lamb was killed for each Israelite family so its blood could be smeared over their doorways to save them from the Angel of Death. In Jesus, the true Passover lamb has finally arrived. He's about to be slaughtered so that by his spilled blood, his chosen people can be saved from death for all eternity. See how the Old Testament symbols beautifully point us to God's plan to save the world through Jesus? Jesus is celebrating Passover with his friends, knowing that the very next day he is literally going to become the sacrificial lamb, finally fulfilling all of the Old Testament prophecies.

The garden of Gethsemane

After dinner, Jesus and the disciples went out to a garden called Gethsemane to pray. He's in absolute agony emotionally, thinking about what's going to happen to him. Verse 38 says he's so overwhelmed by his sorrow that he feels like he's about to die. This is a side of Jesus we've never seen before, and it's devastating. In his weakness and sadness, his response is to run straight to his Father. He prepares to fight the hardest battle of his life by falling to his knees with his face on the ground for hours. When your world feels like its collapsing around you, is your first instinct to take your breaking heart straight to your heavenly Father in prayer?

Jesus' prayers in the garden of Gethsemane are very simple, but they're the most powerful prayers in the entire Bible. We can see so much of Jesus' heart in the words he speaks during his darkest hour. The first time he prays, in verse 39, Jesus asks God to rescue him from the suffering that's ahead of him. Even though this is the plan for salvation that God the Father made with God the Son and God the Holy Spirit before the world began, and even though his whole 33 years on earth have been leading up to this exact moment, Jesus is asking to change the plan at the last minute. He's begging for God to save his chosen people some other way. He's dreading what comes next. But even in his deepest fear and sadness, Jesus says, "Yet not as I will, but as you will" (verse 39). With these incredible words, he's saying to God, "You do what you want to do. I trust your plan. I trust that you know what's best. I trust that you are good. I trust that you love me. I trust that you have a very good reason for whatever happens next."

When we're in the middle of suffering, it's not wrong to pray that God will take the pain away. It is not wrong to ask for healing or to beg for our situation to change. We don't have to pretend we aren't afraid or sad. More than a third of all the psalms are desperate, heartbroken cries for rescue. Some of them even express anger at God! We should bring everything we're thinking and feeling and honestly share it all with God. He loves us, and he wants us to bring our burdens before him, to cry out before him.

However, Jesus' prayer also teaches us that we should pray with the genuine acceptance that God's best answer for us might be, "No." Maybe he won't bring us healing. Maybe his plan isn't to take away our suffering right now, or possibly ever in this life. And if his answer is no, it isn't because he doesn't love us or isn't a good Father. We have to learn how to truly mean those difficult words that Jesus prayed: "Do what you know is best God, I trust you."

The second and third times Jesus prays, in verses 42 and 44, his words have slightly changed. He stops asking for the plan to be changed. It seems like God's already responded to his first prayer and shown him there is no other way for the salvation of the world to happen. God's best answer was, "No." So now Jesus is saying, "If this has to happen, may it happen the way you want." He's praying for the strength to see the mission through to the end. For the ability to persevere through the suffering. For the power to be obedient to God's plan. He's praying that he'll be able to honor God by doing his will, no matter how hard it gets. Beautifully, the parallel version of this event in Luke 22 tells us that God answers by sending an angel to strengthen him. It doesn't stop the anguish Jesus is feeling, and he continues crying his heart out on his knees before God, but it's a wonderful reminder that our Father hears and cares and responds.

In Jesus' simple but heartfelt prayers, we get a glimpse of the most intimate relationship in all of creation. We see that in the hardest moment of his life, Jesus runs straight to his Father. We see the trust Jesus has in his Father's wisdom and love, no matter what happens. We see God the Son willingly submit to God the Father, no matter what it costs him. And in it all, we see the love God has for us, that he would voluntarily make such a unimaginable sacrifice to rescue us from our sin.

Reflect and respond

1. *When your world feels like its collapsing around you, what's your first response and why?*
2. *Why is God trustworthy? What do you know about him that shows he's worthy of all your trust?*

My Father,
You know what I'm struggling with right now.
If it's possible, please rescue me from this situation.
Please take away this hardship.
Yet not as I will, but as you will.
I can only see a tiny part of the situation; you can see the whole story.
I trust your plan for my life.
I trust that you know what's best.
I trust that your timing is perfect.
I trust that you are good and wise.
I trust that you love me.
I trust that even if you say "No" to this prayer today, you have a very good reason for whatever happens next.
Teach me to trust you more.
I surrender all that I am to you, Father.

In Jesus' name,
Amen

Meditation verse for the day:

"My Father, if it is possible, may this cup be taken from me.
Yet not as I will, but as you will."
(Matthew 26:39)

Day 59

Jesus is Always Faithful

(READ MATTHEW 26:47–75)

Jesus arrested

THIS SCENE IN THE garden when Jesus gets arrested is amazing. Remember, Jesus has just spent a few hours crying out to God in sorrow and anguish, his heart breaking. But now he suddenly seems to be in a completely different head-space! He's calm and confident, thoughtful and strong. He gently calls Judas "friend", even while Judas is in the process of betraying him. He scolds one of his followers for attacking a man in self-defence and cutting off his ear. The parallel story in John 18 tells us it was Peter who swung the sword, and another perspective on the event in Luke 22 includes that Jesus even healed the man's ear afterwards. He literally healed one of the enemies who had come to put him to death!

It's very clear all the way through this scene that Jesus is on a mission. He's focused and determined to do what he has to do. It might seem to his followers like everything's falling apart, but he's in control. He knows that he could call it off at any time and be instantly surrounded by armies of angels (verse 53), but he's made the choice to obey his Father and see this plan through to the bitter end. God has answered Jesus' earlier prayer and given him the strength and courage to face this suffering boldly. His trust in his Father overrides any fear or sadness that might threaten to overwhelm him, and he has peace in his heart about what is coming next. He willingly and lovingly faces the cross for us.

Peter disowns Jesus

Let's focus now on Peter. His night has been a rollercoaster! He started the evening celebrating the Passover with his closest friends, then went to the garden to pray with Jesus. Along the way, Jesus prophesied that Peter would abandon him that very night. Peter didn't want to believe it, and argued in verse 35 that he would die for Jesus! But just moments later when Jesus was distraught, Peter couldn't even manage to stay awake for an hour to support him as he prayed. He probably felt pretty guilty that he'd disappointed his beloved rabbi. And yet, when Jesus went away to pray a second time, Peter fell asleep again. He let Jesus down twice in a row. Maybe that's why he responds so aggressively when Jesus is getting arrested, chopping a guy's ear off with his sword. Perhaps he was just trying to prove that he had Jesus' back, and show that he wouldn't abandon him.

After Jesus is arrested, verse 56 tells us that all the disciples run away and leave him, including Peter. As he ran in fear his heart must have sunk in shame, remembering what Jesus had predicted earlier that night. Later that evening in the chief priest's courtyard, Peter finally denies that he even knows Jesus. Not once, not twice, but three times. And he doesn't just do it casually; he swears! He promises! He curses!

Then the rooster crows and Peter realizes that what Jesus prophesied about him has come true. The parallel version of this story in Luke's Gospel includes a devastating detail here. It says Jesus is in the same area, being guarded by soldiers. He can hear Peter yelling and swearing that they don't know each other. Luke 22:61 says that as Peter denied Jesus for the third time, "the Lord turned and looked straight at Peter." They have eye contact. These two best friends, who have spent nearly every moment of the past three years together, lock eyes across the courtyard. No wonder Peter ran outside the gate and wept bitterly at what he had done.

Peter, the most confident and outgoing of Jesus' followers, feels like a complete failure. In just one tragic night he's let Jesus down over and over and over. It's easy for us to judge Peter for being so weak and fearful, but thankfully most of us will never be in his position. If your life were at risk for standing with Jesus, would you deny him too?

The story isn't finished

Fortunately for Peter (and for us), this isn't the end of his story. As we keep reading through the New Testament, we find out that Peter eventually becomes the leader of the twelve apostles (which is the new name for the disciples.) Just fifty days after Jesus' death, Peter is the first apostle to preach publicly to the crowds in Acts 2, and he is also the first to do a miracle in Jesus' name in Acts 3. All the way through Acts, Peter boldly and courageously teaches about Jesus in front of huge crowds, including the religious leaders. He's arrested and beaten multiple times, but continues to confidently preach the good news, leading thousands of people to trust in Jesus. Peter, the uneducated fisherman, even ended up being the author of a few books in the New Testament! As Jesus prophesied about him in Matthew 16:18, Peter became the firm, faithful rock on which the Christian church's foundations were built.

What an incredible story of transformation and redemption! Peter's life shows us that we can never mess up too much for God. No matter how badly we let him down, he's faithful to us. No matter how much we feel like we've failed, God still wants to use us in his story. No matter who we are or what we've done, it's never too late for God to turn our lives around. Jesus knew all along that Peter would deny him right when it mattered most, and he still loved him. Jesus stayed faithful to Peter no matter how many times Peter was unfaithful to Jesus.

The key to understanding Peter's amazing transformation is in Luke 22:31–32. Right before Jesus tells Peter he'll deny him three times, he says this: "Satan has asked to sift all of you as wheat. But I have prayed for you Simon, that your faith may not fail. And when you have turned back, strengthen your brothers." (Remember that Peter's name is Simon Peter, which is why Jesus sometimes calls him Simon.) Jesus is telling Peter that he has been praying for him all along. Before Peter even realized that Satan was attacking his faith, Jesus knew and was already praying for him. The Bible calls Jesus our perfect high priest, our advocate before the throne of God. This means he stands between God and us, representing our needs and speaking up on our behalf.

How wonderful it is to know that we aren't fighting our spiritual battles on our own! Jesus is fighting on our side. He's bringing our situation before God, asking the Father to protect us. And even if we fail the tests of faith over and over and over, Jesus is always faithful to us. He knows how to weave our deepest failures into his beautiful story of hope, making something beautiful out of our messes. And then he gives us opportunities to encourage others with our testimony, redeeming our greatest disasters for the good of ourselves and others.

Reflect and respond

1. What do you need to repent for this week, turning back to God?
2. Reflect on the way Jesus is always advocating for you before the throne of God the Father. Why is this so precious and encouraging to you?

Almighty God,
You are the God of new beginnings.
You give sight to the blind, and healing to the sick.
You fill the empty to overflowing, and you gently bandage up the broken-hearted.
You replace ashes with a crown of beauty, and replace mourning with joy.
You welcome outsiders and sinners into your glorious story of redemption.
You use messy, broken people like Peter and me for the glory of your name.
You knew all of my sin and shame, and you still rescued me.
But in your abundant grace and mercy and goodness, you don't leave me the way you found me.
Your Spirit is helping me repent and turn back to you, over and over.
Your Spirit is building my faith so that I can stand up boldly for you.
Rewrite my story so that you get the glory, my Lord and my Redeemer.

In Jesus' name,
Amen

Meditation verse for the day:

But the Lord is faithful, and he will strengthen you
and protect you from the evil one.
(2 Thessalonians 3:3)

Day 60

Pilate and Barabbas

(READ MATTHEW 27:1–26)

IT'S VERY EARLY ON Friday morning, the day of Jesus' death. The religious leaders drag Jesus before the Roman governor Pontius Pilate, because they don't have the authority to sentence him to death. Pilate's job as governor is to make sure the locals don't cause any trouble for Rome, and what we see happening in these verses is a strategic political game. Pilate can see Jesus is innocent and doesn't deserve to die, but he needs to make the local religious leaders happy. He knows they're just jealous of Jesus, but he needs to keep the peace so that he keeps his job. He enjoys being in power, and doesn't want to lose it.

Another version of this event in Luke 23 tells us Pilate tries everything he can to find a way to let Jesus go. He gives Jesus opportunities to defend himself, but Jesus doesn't take them. He tries to handball the problem to another local ruler, Herod, but Herod just sends Jesus back. Then Pilate tries to use the annual Passover tradition of letting a prisoner free as a way of avoiding this difficult decision. He lets the crowd choose between Jesus and a murderer, assuming they'll decide Jesus should be the one to go free. But he underestimates the influence of the religious leaders, who convince the crowd to ask for Barabbas the murderer to go free instead! Pilate is obviously running out of ideas, feeling the pressure from the local leaders to do what they want. In the end, he reluctantly hands Jesus over to the soldiers to be crucified even though he knows it's wrong.

The ultimate authority

To anyone watching this trial, it must have seemed like a very bad situation for Jesus. He's tied up and badly beaten, standing alone in front of the governor. Pilate has all the power and might of the largest empire on earth behind him. Jesus doesn't speak up for himself or try to explain the situation. He doesn't seem to want to defend himself at all. However, another parallel version of this interaction in John 19:10–11 includes this conversation:

> PILATE: Do you refuse to speak to me? Don't you realize I have power either to free you or to crucify you?
>
> JESUS: You would have no power over me if it were not given to you from above.

Jesus is boldly telling the most powerful man in the whole region that all his authority comes from God. God put Pilate in this job for this exact reason. God has a plan that Pilate doesn't know about, and he's using Pilate to make it happen. Pilate thinks he's in charge here, but God is really the one in control of the story.

This is powerful encouragement for every single one of us as we face hard times in life. We might look at our situation and think it's hopeless. We might feel like it's completely out of control, or wonder what good could ever come out of it. Our enemies might seem too big, too strong, too powerful. We might feel too weak, too scared, too alone. But we have to constantly remind ourselves that behind the scenes our loving Father is ultimately in control. He is sovereign. He is bigger than our worst enemy or our greatest struggle. He has a plan which he has been putting into action piece by piece since the beginning of creation. Unlike Jesus, we usually don't understand the plan until much, much later (or sometimes not until we get to heaven). But if we trust that God has the ultimate authority in the universe, we can face our suffering with the same peace in our hearts that Jesus had, no matter what happens.

We are Barabbas

All four Gospels tell different parts of the story of Jesus' life, depending on which particular things their Holy Spirit-led authors thought were most important. It's interesting that even though all four Gospels don't even include the story of Jesus' birth, they *do* all include a mention of Barabbas. For some reason, this random violent criminal stood out to each Gospel's author as being important enough to include in their writings. Perhaps God planned it that way to highlight that the story of Barabbas is actually the story of all of us.

Barabbas was a rebel and a murderer who fought to overthrow the Roman Empire. He was in jail for crimes he *had* committed, so his sentence was just and right according to the law. He deserved his punishment. Jesus was innocent. He was completely blameless. He was falsely accused. And yet Jesus traded places with Barabbas. The criminal was set free to live again by the death of this completely innocent man. Jesus died in his place.

We are all rebels like Barabbas. We want to rule ourselves, and live life according to our own wisdom and desires. We all reject God's right to have authority over our lives. This means we fully deserve the judgment that's coming our way. God doesn't owe us anything. And yet in his love for us, Jesus shows us unimaginable mercy by volunteering to lay down his perfect life for us, to be punished on our behalf, and to receive the death that should rightfully be ours. We're set free through his sacrifice. We're given life through his death. What a Savior! What amazing grace!

Reflect and respond

1. When you're in the middle of a crisis, what kind of things do you think about God?
2. Next time you're in the middle of a crisis, how can you encourage your heart and mind to trust that God is in control? What can you remind yourself about his character and his power?

Lord of All,
I desperately want to be in control of my own life.
I feel fear and anxiety if I can't make things go my way.
I want the world to revolve around my idea of what is right and fair and wise.
It's so hard for me to surrender my need for control to you.
Forgive me for rejecting your rightful authority over me.
Help me to trust you like Jesus did in his darkest hour.
Help me to remember that you have all authority on earth and in heaven.

In Jesus' name,
Amen

Meditation verse for the day:

You would have no power over me
if it were not given to you from above.
(John 19:11)

Day 61

The Crucifixion

(Read Matthew 27:27–50)

The humble Savior

When you think about a cross, what do you picture? Jewellery? A tattoo? A stained-glass window? Cross symbols have become so normal in Western culture that we often don't realize what a terrible death crucifixion was in Jesus' time. For the ancient readers of Matthew's Gospel, it would have been shocking and scandalous for someone like Jesus to die on a cross.

Back then, crucifixion was considered too shameful for Roman citizens or rich and powerful people, so it was saved only for the lowest criminals and slaves. The famous ancient Roman writer Cicero described it as the most extreme, horribly cruel punishment possible, even more gruesome than being burned alive or decapitated. It was specially designed to be a slow, painful death. Criminals hung from huge nails in their wrists for days, dying slowly in extreme agony as they struggled for every breath. It was also a public death. Criminals were hung in places where they could be mocked and ridiculed by people passing by, and where they could serve as a warning for others who might be tempted to rebel against Rome. It was a death designed to be as humiliating and dishonorable as possible.

Jesus did not have to die on that cross. He lovingly chose to die there to for me and for you, because it was the only way to save us. Let that sink in. The all-powerful Son of God who has existed from before time began, through whom everything that exists was created, and who has armies of angels under his command, chose to die the most shameful, painful death possible for us. He was not put there by soldiers and held there by nails; he put himself up on that cross voluntarily and was held there by his deep love for us. He had the power to come down at any time, but he didn't. And when the very people he was dying for walked past his cross and mocked him, he didn't say a word back. This is our loving, humble Savior.

Why have you forsaken me?

As awful as it was, the pain and public humiliation of crucifixion was not actually the worst thing for Jesus that day. When he was crying out to God in the garden of Gethsemane the night before, it probably wasn't the physical torture ahead of him that was the main thing on his mind. 2 Corinthians 5:21 tells us that on the cross Jesus *became* sin for us. He took on all of the sins of world, and then God punished him as if those sins were his own. This means that Almighty God's terrifying, holy anger poured out onto Jesus on the cross. An eternity worth of judgment and damnation that should have been coming at me and you and billions of others was directed towards Jesus instead, all in one instant.

Remember back when we were reading Matthew 17 and we learned about the beautiful love between the Trinity? For all of eternity past, God the Father, Son and Holy Spirit have existed in a state of pure love towards one another, like a never-ending dance. They glorify and honor one another in complete adoration and fullness of joy, all day every day, forever and ever. But for Jesus on the cross that day, all of the disgusting, horrific sins of humanity suddenly came in between himself and his beloved Father. My own selfishness and rebellion interrupted that eternal love dance. Your sins were there too. Along with billions of others. So what was worse for Jesus that day than the incredible pain of being nailed to a cross and slowly suffocating to death? Experiencing the extreme spiritual agony of being the target of God's righteous wrath. Experiencing separation from the Father he had spent the whole of existence being extravagantly loved by.

In verse 46 Jesus cries out, "My God, my God, why have you forsaken me?" Forsaken means to be abandoned or completely alone. Jesus doesn't say this because he's forgotten his mission, or doesn't understand what's happening to him. He was prepared for exactly this. It's a passionate cry of horror from the deepest part of his spirit. For the first time in all eternity, he feels abandoned by God. He feels judged by God. He feels nothing but God's holy anger against sin. He feels like he's lost the loving relationship with his Father that's been the greatest delight of his entire existence. We'll never be able to understand how crushing that devastation was to his soul.

Psalm 22

The words Jesus cries out in verse 46 are more than just the heartfelt desperation of a suffering man. They're actually a quote from Psalm 22. This Psalm was written by King David about a thousand years before Jesus' birth. Even though David wouldn't have known it at the time, the Holy Spirit was influencing him to write words that hinted at Jesus' future sacrifice on the cross. Jesus' death echoes many parts of Psalm 22, including that his hands and feet were pierced, and that people cast lots for his clothes.

Jesus' quote from Psalm 22 is actually really encouraging to us. It reminds us again that God planned in advance what would happen to Jesus, and that everything was going exactly according to that plan. Not even the smallest detail of what happened that day was an accident. Evil had not won. God was still in control, even though it might not have seemed like it to anyone watching in that horrific moment. And as Jesus himself knew very well, Psalm 22 starts with a desperate cry for help but ends with joyful confidence in God. The last ten verses of the psalm ring out with praises to God, proclaiming that he is righteous and sovereign and that he'll always rescue those who cry out to him for help. On the cross Jesus feels the full weight of God's terrible judgment against sin, but even in his deepest pain he trusts that God's plan will turn out to be wonderfully good.

Reflect and respond

1. *How has today's devotions made you more grateful for Jesus' sacrifice for you?*
2. *What did God show you of his sovereignty (control over everything) through today's devotions?*

God my Redeemer,
Thank you for Jesus.
Thank you for his obedience and humility and love.
Thank you that he willingly took the pain and suffering I deserve, to bring me peace with you.
Thank you for loving me so much that you gave what was most precious to you: your beloved Son.
Thank you that you are sovereign even in the worst situations, when it looks like all hope is lost and evil has won.
I want to sing your praises with every breath I have.
I love you!

In Jesus' name,
Amen

Meditation verse for the day:

We all, like sheep, have gone astray,
each of us has turned to our own way;
and the Lord has laid on him the iniquity of us all.
(Isaiah 53:6)

Day 62

The Importance of Jesus' Death

(Read Matthew 27:45–66)

Pretty much all ancient and modern historians believe Jesus was a real historical figure. Muslims believe he was a prophet, and many Jews think he was a good moral teacher. Even lots of non-Christians respect the teachings of Jesus and the way he lived his life. They agree that he was a kind, wise leader. But if we only focus on how Jesus lived and what he taught, we're missing the most important part of his story. If we only admire Jesus as a loving teacher and a good person, we're not actually saved. To receive eternal salvation, we have to believe that Jesus died on the cross to be punished for our sins. We have to trust that his perfect sacrifice on our behalf is the only way we're made righteous before God. He has to be our Savior, not just someone we respect. His death is what his whole life was for!

The death of Jesus was the single most important day in the history of the world. It's the climax of the Bible, the main event that the entire story has been building up to. In 1 Corinthians 1:23 Paul says that the whole gospel message can be summed up in two words: Christ crucified. It's as simple as that. We read about the importance of the cross all the way through the rest of the New Testament. So let's make sure we understand exactly why Jesus' death is such a huge deal for us as Christians.

The symbolism of the temple

In verses 45–53, we read that some supernatural things happen, which is exactly what you'd expect when the Son of God is killed. The sun goes dark for three hours in the middle of the day, there's an earthquake that splits open tombs and some dead people come back to life, and the huge curtain in the temple is torn in half from top to bottom. The symbolism of the temple curtain tearing gives us a wonderful answer to the question of why Jesus' death is so important, but to fully understand what it means we have to go back to the Old Testament.

Theologian Don Carson explains that the temple is a central theme that threads through the entire Bible, from Genesis to Revelation. He describes the temple as the "meeting place between God and people."[1] When we're reading the Old Testament, most of us get bored and skip over the detailed instructions God gives the Israelites for how to build the tabernacle (which was the very first temple.) We feel like it isn't relevant what woods and fabrics it was made of, or the exact measurements of each area, or how many golden lamps and plates there were. But we're missing out! There's so much incredible meaning behind every detail of the temple's construction. Understanding the symbolism literally built into the temple helps us see the holiness of God more clearly. If you're interested in learning more about it all, Bible teacher Beth Moore has a fantastic study called *A Woman's Heart* (written for women, but helpful for everyone.)

The curtain

For today though, we just need to focus on the curtain, which is also called the veil. This beautiful, heavy curtain is described in Exodus 26:31–33. It was hung in the entrance to the Most Holy Place, which was also called the Holy of Holies. This was the inner sanctuary of the temple, where the presence and glory of God was. It was an incredibly sacred space. No human was allowed to enter the Holy of Holies or they would die, with the exception of the high priest. Once a year on the Day of Atonement (still celebrated by Jewish people today as Yom Kippur), the high priest had to be purified by ritually washing and dressing, before passing through the curtain to sprinkle sacrificial animal blood in the Holy of Holies. This is how the Israelites received forgiveness for their sins.

---

1. Carson, "Understand the Temple".

The Importance of Jesus' Death

This might sound strange to us these days, but God had a purpose in it. It was all designed to teach the Israelites how unimaginably holy God is. They couldn't just come into his presence on their own terms, any time or any way they liked. He's too holy for that. Their sinfulness meant they weren't worthy to come near him. They needed a special high priest to go on their behalf. They needed to sacrifice something valuable and pure to demonstrate their repentance, and to humbly ask for God's forgiveness. They needed to take him *extremely* seriously. They needed to treat him with great reverence. The thick curtain symbolized that there was a huge separation between God and his people, between clean and unclean, between sacred and sinful.

Just like most of the things in the Old Testament, all of this was also a picture of the future Messiah who was coming to save the Israelites. Jesus fulfils all of the purposes of the original temple perfectly. He's now our great high priest, representing us before God. He's also the perfect sacrifice made once and for all, for the forgiveness of our sins. Through Jesus' death we've been forgiven and made righteous, so we can come into God's holy presence. Through the blood of Jesus, we've been reconciled to God, brought back into a relationship with him. When Jesus died, the curtain tore to show that we can now access God freely through Jesus. We aren't separated from him anymore. We've been made clean and holy. Hebrews 10:19–20 describes it like this: "We have confidence to enter the Most Holy Place by the blood of Jesus, by a new and living way opened for us through the curtain, that is, his body."

So this is why the death of Jesus matters so much to us as Christians. This is why we call the day commemorating Jesus' horrific death *Good* Friday. This is why we sing songs at church about how precious the blood of Jesus is. Because without his death, our sin would still be separating us from God. Without his sacrifice, there would still be a heavy curtain holding us back from God's presence. But when Jesus died on that cross, everything changed. The veil was torn! Our sins were forgiven. We're now invited to come before the throne of the Lord of Creation without fear. He delights in welcoming us into his presence. Hallelujah!

Reflect and respond

1. What part of today's devotions encouraged you the most, and why?
2. Reflect for a moment on God's perfect holiness. How does this challenge you to change your attitude or perspective when you come into his presence in prayer and worship?

Father God,
You've been making a way for unworthy humans to come into your holy presence for all of time.
Thank you that through the blood of Jesus I can come to you as your child, and be confident in your love for me.
I can never thank you enough.

In Jesus' name,
Amen

Meditation verse for the day:

Since we have confidence to enter the Most Holy Place by the blood of Jesus, by a new and living way opened for us through the curtain . . . and since we have a great high priest over the house of God, let us draw near to God with a sincere heart and the full assurance that faith brings.
(Hebrews 10:19–22)

Day 63

The Resurrected King

(Read Matthew Chapter 28)

There's only one event in history that might possibly be greater than Jesus' death: his resurrection. Paul writes in 1 Corinthians 15:14 that "if Christ has not been raised [back to life], our preaching is useless and so is your faith." He's saying that Christianity means absolutely nothing if Jesus hasn't risen from the dead.

Without the resurrection, Jesus could have just been a good man who had delusions that he was the Son of God. Without the resurrection, we'd have no evidence that he actually overcame death for us. We'd have no confidence in his promise that we'll also be resurrected to reign with him for all eternity. But the resurrection is proof that he is who he says he is. He is the Messiah! He is the Son of God! He is the Savior of the world! And he has taken our sin and shame and given us his own perfect righteousness in its place.

The Great Commission

Matthew 28 doesn't give us lots of information about what Jesus did after his resurrection. Both Luke and John include much more detailed descriptions of the hundreds of people he saw and the proof he gave them that he was really alive, and Acts 1 tells us that after 40 days he was taken up into heaven. But even though it's a short passage, Matthew 28 does include some incredibly important words from Jesus that should have a huge impact on our lives.

Jesus' instructions in verse 19 to his remaining eleven disciples are often called the Great Commission. A commission is a command. Jesus commands his disciples to "go and make disciples of all nations". He makes it clear that the gospel is good news for *everybody*. All nations. All cultures and languages and ethnicities. Everyone everywhere is welcome in the family of God. Jesus tells the disciples to baptize these new Christians and teach them how to understand and obey everything that Jesus taught. If you're a Christian, this command is for you, too. It's literally the life-long mission that God has personally given you. If you're wondering what you're meant to be doing with your life, this is the answer!

We aren't called to be followers of Jesus just to quietly keep our salvation and joy to ourselves. We aren't meant to just put our feet up and relax now that we've got eternity all figured out. We also aren't here on earth to simply enjoy all the pleasures of this world like everyone around us. Becoming a Christian means that God expects a response from us. Our main job while Jesus is gone is to teach people to get to know him and find their deepest joy in him. We're meant to help people obey Jesus' commands: to love God and love others. He won't be gone forever, and when he comes back it'll be too late. He wants every single one of us to play a role in the mission to save his lost sheep before he returns to judge the world. What an honor! What a responsibility!

What this means is that we're all missionaries. We're doing holy work, all the time, wherever God's placed us. No age is too young or too old. You can be a missionary in your school or workplace or family. Artists are missionaries, doctors are missionaries, mechanics are missionaries, retired folk are missionaries, bricklayers are missionaries, accountants are missionaries, stay-at-home-parents are missionaries. If you're a Christian, you're called to be a missionary until the day you die.

The authority and presence of Jesus

Jesus has said some really hard things about what it means to be his followers. We might have to sacrifice everything, even our lives. We have to die to who we used to be. We have to love others until it hurts. We have to carry our cross and follow him. Jesus isn't saying our mission will be easy and fun all the time. He's not promising it will be successful in the ways we expect. In fact, he promises we'll suffer just like he did. There will be many times when we feel like our mission is hopeless. There will be days when the darkness in the world feels like it will overwhelm us. There will be devastating times when it seems like the devil has won the war. There will be depressing times when we feel like failures or frauds.

But there's some really encouraging news that comes along with this challenging commission. The first is in verse 18. Jesus says the reason we should go out and make disciples is that he's been given "all authority in heaven and on earth." He's reminding us that he's in control. He is Lord. He's sovereign over the entire universe and every human and spirit in it. He's sending us out into the world to do work for him, but he's already prepared in advance what that work will be, and will give us everything we need to do it. Thankfully, the salvation of the people around us doesn't all depend on us getting everything right ourselves. He'll be our strength. He'll guide us and teach us. He'll fight our battles for us. He'll soften people's hearts so that they can hear the message of hope we're sharing. He's inviting us to help plant the seeds of the gospel, but he's the one who'll make sure those seeds grow. That's why he's called the Author of Faith, not us. As Mother Teresa said, "God has not called me to be successful . . . God has called me to be faithful."[1] We're responsible for being faithful to the mission that God has given us, but the results are in his hands. What particular mission field is God calling you to be faithful in?

The second great piece of encouragement Jesus gives us is in verse 20: "And surely I am with you always, to the very end of the age." What incredible words for Matthew to end his Gospel with! Soon after saying this Jesus ascended into heaven to sit at the right hand of God, so clearly he didn't mean he's with us physically. But his presence is with each of us, every breath we take. His Spirit lives inside us. He'll never leave or forsake us. God is with us always. Whether we feel him or not, we have his full attention every moment. This is actually a message God gives his people every step of the way through the Bible: *Do not fear, for I am with you*. He says it to the Israelites when they're facing their scariest moments. He says it to his prophets when they doubt themselves. He says it to the Apostle Paul when he's facing death. And he said it to the whole world when he sent his Son to us as Immanuel, *God with us.*

Our mission will be hard. However, if we always remember that Jesus is with us every step of the way, and that he has all power on heaven and earth, it completely changes our perspective. We're fighting on the winning side, doing the work of Almighty God! When God is for us, who can stand

---

1. Spink, *Mother Teresa*, 245.

against us? So let's faithfully share the love of Jesus and confidently leave the results in his hands. It may cost us everything. But Jesus, the beautiful treasure of our hearts, is worth it all.

Reflect and respond

1. What mission field has God put you in right now? Who are the specific people in your life who need to hear about the love of Jesus?
2. How do Jesus' promises of his sovereignty and his presence encourage and empower you to be a bold missionary for him?

Sovereign Lord,
You brought me from death to life, and set me free from slavery to sin!
You have called me your child, and welcomed me into your holy presence!
You rejoice over me with singing!
Thank you Father.
I give my life to you as a living sacrifice.
Please use me.
Please make my life a testimony to the glorious splendour of your majesty.
Lord, help me share your love with the people around me.
Remind me that you have all authority in heaven and on earth.
Remind me that you are with me always.
May my whole life be a love song to you.

In Jesus' name,
Amen

Meditation verse for the day:

All authority in heaven and on earth has been given to me.
Therefore go and make disciples of all nations, baptizing them
in the name of the Father and of the Son and of the Holy Spirit,
and teaching them to obey everything I have commanded you.
And surely I am with you always, until the very end of the age.
(Matthew 28:18–20)

Bibliography

Carson, Don. "Why We Must Understand the Temple in God's Plan Today." Desiring God, October 21, 2021. https://www.desiringgod.org/interviews/why-we-must-understand-the-temple-in-gods-plan-today.

Chambers, Oswald. "The Key of the Greater Work." My Utmost for His Highest, October 21, 2021. https://utmost.org/the-key-of-the-greater-work.

Chan, Francis. *Letters to the Church.* Colorado Springs: David C Cook, 2018.

Elliot, Elisabeth, ed. *The Journals of Jim Elliot.* Grand Rapids, MI: Revell, 1978.

Hill Perry, Jackie. *Jude: Contending for the Faith in Today's Culture.* Nashville: Lifeway, 2020.

Keller, Timothy. *Counterfeit Gods: When the Empty Promises of Love, Money and Power Let You Down.* London: Hodder & Stoughton, 2009.

———. *Hidden Christmas: The Surprising Truth Behind the Birth of Christ.* London: Hodder & Stoughton, 2016.

———. *Romans 1–7 For You.* United Kingdom: The Good Book Company, 2014.

———. (@timkellernyc). "There are some needs only you can see." Twitter, August 14, 2021, 2:33 AM. https://twitter.com/timkellernyc/status/1426250454107885571.

Lewis, C. S. *The Weight of Glory and Other Addresses.* New York: The Macmillan Company, 1949.

Moore, Beth. "The Captivated Mind." In *Passion: The Bright Light of Glory*, edited by Louie Giglio, 49–59. Nashville: Thomas Nelson, 2014.

Ortlund, Dane. *Gentle and Lowly: The Heart of Christ for Sinners and Sufferers.* Wheaton: Crossway, 2020.

Packer, J. I. *Knowing God.* London: Hodder and Stoughton, 1978.

Piper, John. "Are You Just Using Jesus?" Desiring God, November 14, 2021. https://www.desiringgod.org/messages/right-with-god-right-with-man/excerpts/are-you-just-using-jesus.

———. *Don't Waste Your Life.* Wheaton: Crossway, 2003.

———. "Love Your Neighbor as Yourself, Part 1." Desiring God, December 16, 2021. https://www.desiringgod.org/messages/love-your-neighbor-as-yourself-part-1

Ramsey, Adam. *Truth on Fire: Gazing at God Until Your Heart Sings.* Turkey: The Good Book Company. 2021.

Spink, Kathryn. *Mother Teresa: An Authorized Biography.* New York: HarperOne, 2011.

Tozer, A. W. *The Knowledge of the Holy.* New York: HarperOne, 1961.

Tyson, Jon. "Disruptive Discipleship—An Overview: Flourishing in the Kingdom." Sermon, City of the Church of New York, New York, filmed September 20, 2020. Video of sermon, 1:29:12. https://www.church.nyc/wk1-an-overview.

www.ingramcontent.com/pod-product-compliance
Lightning Source LLC
Chambersburg PA
CBHW070244230426
43664CB00014B/2406